The Blotting Paper

Chandan Sukumar Sengupta

ISBN 978-93-5559-187-6
© Chandan Sukumar Sengupta 2021
Published in India 2021 by Pencil

A brand of

One Point Six Technologies Pvt. Ltd.
123, Building J2, Shram Seva Premises,
Wadala Truck Terminal, Wadala (E)
Mumbai 400037, Maharashtra, INDIA
E connect@thepencilapp.com
W www.thepencilapp.com

Author biography

Author is working in the field of Science and Technology since 1995. More than 150 different titles were published through different National as well as International PPublishing houses.

CONTENTS

Preface

The history of Afghanistan dates back to the epics and before the socialisation of people near the Kandahar Valley. It is a landlocked country. It had 31.4 million residents during 2020. The land was invaded periodically by many invadors like Alexander, Aryans, Mughals, Turks, British, Russians and Americans during last 20 years. For a longer time during 19th Century it worked as a buffer state between Great Empires of British and Russians.

Mujahideen rebels were smashed down during 1980s by Russians and the state got its identity in the form of a Socialist Republic. Once again almost all parts of the country were captured by Islamic fundamentalists by the end of 1996. They came in power and rulead as a totalitarian regime for near about five years. Another twist in the history of Afghanistan came in the form of invation of US led NATO forces for smashing down Islamic extremists. Taliban were removed from the power during 2001 but ost of the parts of the country remained in their operational dominance.

Coinciding with the return of US forces Taliban took advantage and implied a hold upon the National Security system. They even compelled the president of that country to leave the capital.

These days the country is experiencing high level of corruption, malpractices and lawlessness. People suffer a lot due to lack of quality food and proper schooling. Women and children of the society are more vulnerable. Their chance of access to law and judiciary is feeble. Once in olden times the place was ruled efficiently by Hindu rulers. During 11th Century Mahmud of Ghajni defeated Hindu rulers and Islamised most of the parts of Afghanistan.

Since olden times the area had experienced different ups and downs and never worked out any unity among them. By the end of 1747 Afghanistan started organising itself under the leadership of Ahmad Shah Durrani. After the death of Durrani the partial wakness in organising security forces was taken up by Sikhs and British. The year 1919 came in the history of Afghanistan which brought complete freedom for the people. The nation soon indulged in a civil war (1928-29) bringing utter unrest for the entire territory.[1] The year 1989 to 1992 was the aother teure of civil war followed by Russian intervention to make it a socialist republic. US led NATO forces entered the scenario during 2001 to make it a democratic republic.

At present some other states are working out a comprehensive plan to enter the national politics. They are also in a mood to explore resources of the country for grabbing it and for utilising it by part for making the life of Afghan people prosperous.

Chandan Sengupta

Author

[1] Muḥammad, Fayz̤; McChesney, R. D. (1999). Kabul under siege: Fayz Muhammad's account of the 1929 Uprising. Markus Wiener Publishers. pp. 39, 40. ISBN 9781558761544. Archived from the original on 4 April 2019. Retrieved 15 June 2019.

Introduction

Afghanistan is becoming a widely discussed issue during the beginning of the 21st century because of the involvement of Osama Bin Laden in organizing a planned attack in USA and the entry of US led NATO in the Afghan arena for smashing extremists down the frame. It was since 2001 onwards that the entire world has witnessed the efforts of NATO for socializing varous rebels of Afghan base. We move back to look upon the historical records after which the glory of Afghan people went on trailing.

India is differently related to the people of Afghanistan in various ways. Once Afghan ruler Sher Shah invaded India main land for defeating Mughals and duly established his empire in Delhi. His capabilities of administration and land reforms system were properly welcomed by historians. Not only had the case of Sher Shah, other rulers of Afghan origin also invaded the India main land and aspired for winning the confidence of local people. History changed its course while keeping pace with modernization and Afghans lost their way in the middle at the beginning of 20th century. They even failed to explore the plenty of resources they had in their mines. Modernization, Industrialisation, mechanization of services sector and rights of girls and women were some of the fields remained neglected even after the World War II.

Countries maintaining cross cultural as well as trade relations with Afghanistan wanted to explore different possibilities of exploring resources for the purpose of accelerating the pace of development. The only obstacle that hampered their advancement was the continuation of conflicts amongst the different settlements of the country.

Afghanistan has been the home to various people. It was also a seat of series of military operations including those made by Alexander, Aryans, Mughals, Arabs, British, Russians and even by US and NATO forces. It remained unconquerable and got a nickname "the graveyard of empires."[1] The name Gandhara, as depicted in the epic The Mahabharata, was the place including parts of Sindh, Punjab and modern Afghanistan. It had military and political associations with Aryans and got a nickname "the Hindu Shahi[2] ." Ultimately the time came during which the first non-military prime minister took the charge of Afghanistan.[3]

The series of battles and other oppressive invasions went on pitching in regularly in the land of prosperity. The conflict went on mushrooming side by side because of infiltration of several intenders of the opportunists.[4] The cost of Soviet invasion was marked in the form of hundreds and thousands of killings and displacements of six million people from their homes.[5] The situation agin tossed differently when US Army and allied NATO troops finalized to quit the land before September 2021. Afghanistan conflict has raised several questions and also compelled us to think about the definite role of the world community towards nullifying the conflict with an instantaneous effort and courage. It also motivated us differently to think about the stand of leading nations towards bringing normalcy in the state.

According to another estimate nearly 400,000 Afghans died during 1990-2001 tenure under various conflicting circumstances.[6] After 2001 scenario, Afghanistan was invaded again to bring Taliban down from the power. This time the leader in the frame of discussion was USA. Their role in Afghanistan was considered as a back-foot race with certain inflictions of mechanizing the warfare of the country. They have decided to quit the runways on or before 31st August 2021 at any cost. It was at the cost of people and currency of Afghanistan. Here also question arises: Is there anything in particular that forced USA to quit? What the role exactly played by China, Russia or Turki in this regard? What format of power politics forced the leading nations to quit the fireplace? Hundreds and thousands of these types of questions can be raised with an objective of tracing out the root cause of the problem which has mounted on the electronic media in the name of Afghanistan and Taliban.

It is not for the first time that Americans worked out a resolution to quit the land of conflicting situation, it is also not for the first time that people of Afghanistan left in the middle at the mercy of God. They had to fight their own people who maintain optimum faith upon arms and warfare. They people also maintain an urge to aspire for an ascent to cope up with the rapid development that the world outside is moving through. People of that country also intend to come up with a people friendly governance which can accommodate aspirations of commune in a broader spectrum. Even after a 20 long years of run up the goal was yet to be set properly. It is known to us now that all the ration bags of Afghani people are filled up with fire crackers and guns. They had only one task to be accomplished: fight against each other and go on practicing armed exercises.

Are the people of Afghanistan really under the tremendous threat because of the mushrooming of armed exercises of rebels from different out-pockets of the country? Are they really under a question mark in terms of their chances of being smashed by the rebels and violent troops of Taliban? Will it give birth to people to people conflict at last?

We will try to find out the issues and concerns related to the armed exercises that got its prominence after the month of August 2021. It was really a fact which drew the attention of the world community and people indulged in calculations by all means to find out the real reason behind the utter failure of a national army in safeguarding people of a country. President of a country quits leaving behind all the other people of a country. Again that person comes back and seeks forgiveness for his conduct. It is the fact which raises questions on the credibility and loyalty of an organized army towards catering services to the citizen of a country. Entire structure of a national security issue came under question mark.

[1] The Graveyard of Empires is a sobriquet associated with Afghanistan. The sobriquet originates from the historical tendency that foreign powers often fail in their invasions of Afghanistan. It is unclear who coined the phrase, and its historical accuracy has been disputed.

[2] Wink, André (2002). Al-Hind, the Making of the Indo-Islamic World: Early Medieval India and the Expansion of Islam 7Th-11th Centuries. BRILL. p. 125. ISBN 0-391-04173-8. Archived from the original on 1 December 2019. Retrieved 11 December 2019.

[3] Eur (2002). The Far East and Australasia 2003. Psychology Press. p. 62. ISBN 978-1-85743-133-9.

[4] "Afghanistan: 20 years of bloodshed". BBC. 26 April 1998. Archived from the original on 17 February 2019. Retrieved 4 July 2019.

[5] "Refugee Admissions Program for Near East and South Asia". Bureau of Population, Refugees, and Migration. Archived from the original on 22 January 2017. Retrieved 29 December 2013.

[6] "Life under Taliban cuts two ways". CSM. 20 September 2001 Archived 30 December 2013 at the Wayback Machine

Power Politics

Polarised Power

Countries around the world started maintaining their difference of opinion regarding the way rebels mounted to smash the national security system and forced a segment of the community to quit instantly. Islamic states maintained difference of opinion regarding the acts of Taliban and started designating it as an act of freedom from the foreign invasion. Countries like China and Turks started exploring an accommodation to get indulge in the reconstruction works after the exit of America. They expressed their eagerness to modify the waves of other country for materialising support for the newly formed government of Afghanistan under the patronage of Taliban. Russia is also playing from the back hand through designing a comprehensive plan of keeping the segment in the hands of neighbouring states. Saudi families wanted to maintain their difference because of their alliance with USA. Israel, the most active state of that locality, got some bad remarks from Taliban and went on finalizing to keep distance from the turmoil. They people also received immediate attention of their Chinese counterparts for regularizing development works.

The dual stand of same group of rebels in different situation raises a question regarding their real objectives behind curtailing the freedom of Press and freedom of women. For what purpose they people want to smash the normal progress of their own community segment? The basic understanding duly inflicted with an objective of practicing religious and cultural extremism can put the entire community in trouble. Normal growth of trade and commerce will be halted. They may fail to compete with the modern trade pattern of the world. The power duly polarized in two different segments has forced the rebels to opt for the extremism duly inflicted with gender bias and falsehood.

Resolute Support Mission (January 2015) launched by NATO was designed to equip Afghan Security Forces differently to equip them for challenges to come. It was the commitment to address the UN Resolution 1378 [1] that compelled USA to come forward and extend support for making Afghan people fit for the modern governance mechanism which is suitable for a state in the modern context. By the end of 2014 the UN Security Council resolved a new stand for establishing peace and normalcy in the country.(Resolution 2189)[2]

Series of development went on across the conflicting situation in the country and the development of the military capabilities of the state was also on its way through incorporation of modern warfare equipment in the barrack of the national armed forces. They also received adequate feedback and training from the peace keepers regarding their efforts of safeguarding people as a whole. They also got adequate technical input from their US counterparts regarding proper and timely uses of modern arm-equipment. They also got an idea to tackle rebels quite efficiently. On the other hand US led peace keepers had to come across a resolution for recognizing the presence of Taliban in the regular line of national security.[3] By the end of April 2020 all political parties of Afghanistan were requested to move forward by casting off their minute differences for the formation of an inclusive government. Intra-Afghan peace effort was on its normal way during September 2020. Ultimately the day came (14th April 2021) to declare a stand of the peace keeping forces to quit the land after transferring the power in the hands of an inclusive government. NATO took another four months to wind up completely from the land of conflict. There developed a concern for appealing the NATO partners for reconsidering their stand in the context of the changing scenario. They wanted NATO and United Nations to re-define their role in Afghanistan for protecting native of the country and for mediating a soft transfer of power. But the commitment of NATO force to leave the land before September 2021 was confirmed.

Retention of Extremism

Extremism of religious and cultural type has become a reality of Afghanistan. Under water current of wishes and willingness of rebels and oppressors are perceivable on the surface. They people started implementing their twenty year long plan to restore the state of Islamic Emirate in Afghanistan. Back history of Taliban made people worry about restoration of normalcy in the state on the basis of the time frame duly prescribed for the purpose.

First indication of the lack of absolute sanction to the growth of extremism in Afghanistan was indicated by Russia in BRICKS summit by suggesting the nation. The Russian leader expected that Afghanistan should not become a threat to its neighbouring countries. It should not support drug trafficking and terrorism.[4] Russia was the only country that expressed its stand broadly in public during a seminar. Rest of the other countries reserved their opinion and preferred adopting the policy of wait and watch. The deal between US and Taliban were implemented after a prolonged tenure of 20 years. It had no positive impact upon the people of that country. They had a bitter experience of the Taliban led government. Their appeal to the world community remained offside during the exit of US from the framework of conflict.

Bringing the normalcy back to its normal schedule is becoming a challenge for the newly formed government of Afghanistan. Governing people under the barrel of arms is really a difficult job to accomplish. It is also difficult to recite words of peace and normalcy in the context of a violent warefare during which a community exhibits their faith on arms and blood-shed. Some of the areas are still fighting Taliban troops for exercising their rights on the land and prosperity. They even declared an open fight for safeguarding themselves from the violent rebels. The violent group clashes and mushrooming of such violent warfare is becoming a regular affair in the land of prosperity. It is becoming more evident from different eventual development in Afghanistan that a government on the force of guns and fire-crackers may not sustain for a longer time. They are simply fighting at the cost of common people.

Aftermath

People of Afghanistan are now free to make themselves free from the violent government by   initiating a peaceful democratic resolution of inclusive administration. The ballot should take the place of bullet. People should impart their opinion in making their nation-state prosperous. People , specially women of Afghanistan, seek support of the international community for making themselves free from the oppression of a violent rebel group. They also want to draw attention of the world community towards the motive force of Taliban in terms of their affinity towards religious extremism. Such extremism will make the community of the country absolutely unfit for getting adjusted with the world community. None of the segments of the Afghan community will support the stand of Taliban regarding the format of a gender biased society.

Elimination of Violence Against Women Law (EVAW) is in the judiciary framework since 2011, but rarely implied adequate stress upon safeguarding women from the mushrooming trend of violence in the country. A major segment of the community maintains their faith in the armed regulation of socialization and acculturation process of children and youths. Barricading women from services sector, keeping them off the regularized track of development and sending them back behind the black curtain are some of such points that exhibited the indication of affinity of the patron of government in that country. Their alignment towards other states of extremism is another fragment of a blotting paper.

EVAW was obviously a landmark legislative instrument meant primarily for combating violence and discriminatory offences against girls and women. Matter becomes a concern when Taliban forces both the parties to resolve their disputes off the judiciary system at a negotiation table. Girls and women are, thus in most of the cases, forced to move on negotiating with the oppressors beyond the scope of EVAW and other allied judiciary frameworks. It is becoming a critical issue day by day and access of women to law is considered as a difficult task in the context of the advancement of Taliban and other extremists towards the governance. The fate of EVAW and other such laws is clear after the finalization of the stand of extremists regarding formation of the Islamic States of Afghanistan.

The constitution itself took its first breathe during 2003. The article 22 became the issue of a fierce debate which ensured the equality of men and women before law. Presidential decree of 2009 brought EVAW in action since 2009. The law and other allied enforcement agencies were there in action since the enactment. This time the survivor of any violence were forced to remain off the judiciary framework. Some sort of complications also persists due to Sharia Law and due to older frameworks of 1976. International human right commitments of the country was aligned to replace the penal code of 1976 with that of 2004. EVAW remained as a specialized penal code provisions during implementation of the legal framework during 2017. Some religious approvals came in the forefront to define the penal code in the line of Sharia provisions. Conservative leaders too maintained their view in favour of the traditional and religious legal frameworks with which some of the other Islamic states are active.

As of August 2021, special courts to implement EVAW provisions are there, may be simply by name, in majority of provinces of Afghanistan.

Hurdles To Justice

It is true that two different types of mind set are in the fore-front in Afghanistan for defining the socialization as well as acculturation process to a greater extent. Enactment of a legal provision itself may not solve the problem of violence against girls and women to a greater extent. If extremists and conservative mind-set gain a lead then we may not expect any enforcement of law like that of EVAW. All the law enforcement agencies come under the clutches of the conservatives and remain off the track to ensure implementation of traditional provisions.

Strong politicians, gang leaders, oppressor groups often take the lead in nullifying the law enforcement agencies and bring them off the track of the judiciary. Policemen also take more time in filing a report and taking any action on the basis of such report is delayed considerably. In majority of cases police often fail to arrest the perpetrators or may remain indulged differently to exhibit loyalty to some strong politicians or headman. Family members and other segment of the relatives rarely support the stand of women during submission of their arguments in the judiciary. Afghan women are less likely to seek any medical aid due to the distant location of service facilities and also due involvement of any unaffordable cost.

Financial dependency and barriers to women living on their own in Afghanistan is another factor which makes the problem a complicated one by exposing such women to oppressors. Security risk is more when women lose their husband or prefer to remain alone in the community. Victims of domestic violence and in-house abuses face tremendous pressure from the family members for remaining off the reach of any legal provisions. Number of cases resolved through mediation was reported beyond 61 percent.[5] Article 39 of EVAW even allows a complainant to withdraw her case for most of the criminalized acts enlisted under EVAW.[6]

In most of the cases EVAW officials assemble a committee comprising representatives from the police, Ministry of Women's Affairs, Justice Ministry, family court, prosecutor's office, and the local office of the human rights commission. They work out a comprehensive plan to record issues and concerns after hearing both the parties and move on to mediate the issue.[7] It will not ascertain any kind of violation of the penal code, but it will even not guarantee the exact law enforcement initiatives for safeguarding rights of girls and women. The matter is still under the question mark when a power backed up by violent groups is in action.

Legal frameworks of any kind may remain un-explored in the context of a violent warfare. It will also hamper the day to day schedule of judiciary and governance. People remain at the mercy of god for exercising each and every particular of their social as well as economic activities.

[1] UN Security Council Resolution (UNSCR) 1378 calls for a central role for the UN in establishing a transitional administration and invites member states to send peacekeepers to Afghanistan. The interim government of Afghanistan wanted UN to play a leading role in establishing peace and normalcy in the country (Year 2002)

[2] The UN Security Council unanimously adopts Resolution 2189, welcoming the new Resolute Support Mission

[3] Secretary General Jens Stoltenberg attends a ceremony held at the President's Palace with Afghan President Ashraf Ghani and US Secretary of Defense Mark Esper, to mark the Joint Declaration between the United States and the Islamic Republic of Afghanistan and signature of an agreement between the United States and the Taliban. The North Atlantic Council welcomes these significant first steps in pursuit of a peaceful settlement and undertakes to implement conditions-based adjustments, including a reduction in military presence.

[4] Afghan territory shouldn't be used to carry out attacks against other nations: BRICS

Without naming any country, the five-nations group also said they reject the double standards in countering terrorism and extremism conducive to terrorism. (The Indian Express , September 09, 2021)

[5] The report prepared by UNAMA.

United Nations Assistance Mission in Afghanistan, Injustice and Impunity Mediation of Criminal Offences of Violence against Women, May 2018, p. 9, https://unama.unmissions.org/sites/default/files/unama_ohchr_evaw_report_2018_injustice_and_impunity_29_may_2018.pdf, accessed July 18, 2021.

[6] EVAW law, article 39: Adjudication of lawsuits and prosecution of perpetrators of crimes stipulated in Articles 22-39 of this law shall be done based on the complaint filed by the victim or her attorney. (b) The victim may withdraw her case at any stage of judicial proceedings (detection, investigation, trial, or conviction) in circumstances mentioned in paragraph 1 of this Article. In this case, the adjudication process and punishment shall be stopped.

[7] Human Rights Watch interview with an EVAW lawyer (name withheld), Kabul, March 23, 2021.

The Other Side of Coin

It is true that both Russia and America experimented a lot in implementing balanced legal provisions in the country. They also indulged in making people of Afghanistan fit enough for the modern format of democratic governance. Russia moved on towards communismic agenda and America moved on towards a democratic agenda. People of Afghanistan remained in dilemma and failed to acquaint themselves properly for any of the structured provisions of governance and judiciary. Reasons may be of different kind, but the prominent one is the alignment of Afghan society towards Islamic provisions. If they maintain a faith in the provisions of Sharia[1], then we also move on to plan something better on the same lines of thought process. Understanding of people of any country or society rarely transforms abruptly without gaining confidence of the community to a greater extent. Situation related to people of Afghanistan is of same type. They got adequate orientations from social , communal as well as democratic and liberal thought process without their adequate alignment towards their religious faith. Because of this reason local leaders kept themselves aside from the main process of transformation.

We cannot imply all the responsibility of a failure in bringing the normalcy back in Afghanistan to Taliban or to

USA alone. If arms are coming in plenty then it is obvious that people maintaining a passion of triggering the same will be also there in plenty. That fact came in reality just after removal of an international military patronage. Failure of the entire military in safeguarding the constitution, judiciary and governance of a country has raised doubts about the strength of the military organization backed by a developed motive force. It has also stunned the world when people came to know about the access of a militant group to the armaments of a country.

It is not an easy access of any extremist group to use the national assets in present day situation without gaining any back hand support from any foreign source. Countries are linked together in terms of networks of monetary policy and markets. They rarely come up to use provisions made by US and other contributors without maintaining an international standard of governance and judiciary. It may be under a strong vigil after Sptember 11,2021 for ensuring the exactness of the governance and judiciary in Afghanistan. Wait and watch policy of countries like India is also inflicted with poor diplomacy and will be considered as a stand inflicted with some sort of escapism. Other far off countries are also conferring frequently to work out a comprehensive plan for safeguarding rights of people living there in utmost misery. Leading nations of Security Council have some other agenda of bringing down extremism by implying a strong sanction on them. The appeal of UN to continue peace talks with extremist group in that country[2] has its own wider implications in the field of international politics when polarized power is taking its reverse spin.

It is now at the disposal of the world community with which they all may work out a resolution to bring normalcy back in the country. History highlihts the ultimate fate of all efforts duly made to lineate people of Afghanistan alongside the international standards of judiciary and governance. Nations inflicted with extremism might expect their own pursuits in the name of the prosperity; similar stand will be taken up by communist as well as democrat leaders of different countries. If any common concern develops under the initiative of any leading poles of power then all other segments might opine to lineate the prosperity of the people of Afghanistan in accord to the standards defined by the leading groups. America as another horizon of a pole is trailing considerably in this race. Their failure to nullify the tension and conflicting situation in and around Kabul has inscribed a set back for the NATO leaders. Prospect and retrospect are yet to be classified for them.

[1] In Arabic, Sharia literally means "the clear, well-trodden path to water". Sharia acts as a code for living that all Muslims should adhere to, including prayers, fasting and donations to the poor. It aims to help Muslims understand how they should lead every aspect of their lives according to God's wishes.

[2] Source: Times Of India, September 10,2021

What We Learn!

All Life is Yoga.

Sri Aurovindo

Conflicting situation may develop any time and at any place. If we consider the modern mechanized warfare then it is becoming evident that modern wars may rarely last for a couple of days, or hardly for a couple of weeks. On the other hand, it will be so devastating that one can rarely traces out the group of warriors indulged differently in that war. This may happen only because of the extreme mechanization of the warfare.

It is also true that we cannot move on mechanizing any warfare anymore because of the involvement of a huge sanction. People, in the modern society, rarely move on for affording a war. They all imply adequate impetus on ensuring the establishment of peace, prosperity and brotherhood in our society. This effort cannot limit its expansion by any border; it can have a normal confluence through countries and states; even it can have adequate hold on the community living throughout the globe.

There are millions of books and narratives with some noble initiative available for explaining and elaborating the propositions of teachings of Gita. Gita is relevant for both learners and teachers. It has something to say even to a layman having less knowledge about the mysteries hidden amidst the conversations displayed in the holy book of Gita.

The term Gita directly links our thinking with the conversation that took place in between Arjun, a Warrior from the side of Pandavas, and his friendly guide Krishna. It was going on amidst a critical situation in which Arjun lost his power of finalising something justifiable to have a sanction of war and killings. A series of killing of such type, in which his beloved ones were at a threshold, made him discontented. Krishna took the role of his charioteer to normalise the situation and to let Arjun understand his own status in a better way. The agitation, as described in the holy book of Mahabharata, was against the stand of his own family members having intention of grabbing all the resources by taking advantage of some conspired game-fares. The game-fare of such type with in infliction of opportunistic ideals were moved on differently and both the segments of a single family took a stand against each other.

Lord Krishna defined his stand by putting himself in the side of Pandavas with a sheer commitment of not to use his weapon at any instances. It was his stand that made him free from direct indulgence of the warfare and made it possible to guard Pandavas through delivering timely relevant instruction. In this way he has secured his position similar to that of the brain in our body. Conversation of

Krishna and Arjun amidst the battle field was also an act of holy instructions duly issued for Arjun to signify his timely need. It had linked senses with duties, established correlation between rights and duties, issued bands of things to be done and things not to be done, entangled a spirit with its higher source, conferred the juxtaposition of creation and the creator and finally re-established need of knowing the self.

It will be even more perfectly balanced to contingent human efforts of ascent towards the state of the unification of conscious mind with that of masterly guide. Effort is also made to encompass the segregation of individual differences from the common philosophical knowledge to make it more people friendly and more relevant, as well as time tested one.

Gita, as a common and popularly contemplated term, indicates towards a subject related to the holy book of Gita having bands of knowledge in the form of a conversation in between Arjun and Krishna. This reality made Gita confined to a limited quarter and placed other holy efforts underneath a shadow of ignorance. We rarely talk about Ram Gita, Sanskaar Gita and some other such efforts having a suffix Gita attached to it.

Gita, in its actual sense, stands for some sort of compilation that people can sing. It can be discussed with some beautiful rhythmic tunes. Collective recitation of Gita brings out a collective wave in the form of auditory vibrations for the purpose of cleansing the immediate surroundings. It also conferred essence of collective and community level worship for making the entire effort possible and for keeping the converged senses of cooperation and brotherhood alive.

To a compilation of prayers and songs meant for the supreme lord the World Poet coined a term "Gitanjali" for it. Linking to the practical aspects of life and mission of an individual with the specified spiritual destiny, Saint Vinoba coined the term "Katha[1] Gita (Gita through a series of stories)" and incorporated all the teachings and narratives of Gita in absolutely friendly way. Examples are in plenty. It had not diffused the glory of the original compilation of Gita, also had not conferred replacing the original poetic compilation with millions of narratives. Waves of vibrations that the chanting of Gita creates is based on the assimilation of collective vibrations of saintly senses that makes a way out through the surrounding of the place of worship and gives birth to an essence of keeping the collective vibrations of cooperation, brotherhood, divine omnipresence and inter-linkages of senses alive.

We, in the same manner, can successfully create hundreds and thousands of such narratives duly inflicted with fundamental human values to make the spark of Gita a confluous one, a vibrant one and a strategic one. It has enormous power of accommodations for incorporating all sorts of socially and culturally relevant directives within the scope of its teaching related to individual refinement impregnated with spiritual ascent. It also makes the relationship of creator and the creation a vibrant one. We can specify any of the particular effort as an initiative inflicted with divine power meant for accomplishing certain works. All such Gita, duly compiled by saintly people, are not with us. In due course of time we have lost many of such beautiful, relevant and time tested compilations due to various reasons. Our mind kept on imbibing presence of such powers tradition by tradition through many of our rituals. Those graceful efforts played a significant role in keeping waves of community worship alive.

Wider dimensions and expanded coverage of the teachings of Gita often make people worried about what to follow and what not to follow in real life. Also in some cases it becomes difficult to think about propositions in the actual ground. Because of lack of timely relevant practical knowledge of the situation, people even keep themselves aside from following and internalising teachings of the holy book in the real life situation. Approach of such religious and cultural teaching, therefore, should have proper considerations of some practical aspects of rituals and worships.

Some people maintain a view regarding Gita is that the entire aspects depicted in this holy book are a confusing one. Saints from olden times worked differently to show that Gita is much relevant in terms of rituals and propositions presented in it. Here also we are trying to trace out a link up in between rituals, traditions and practices that we have in nature to re-establish the age old faiths of the omnipresence of divine within us at its varying formats.

We can see things as they occupy a definite shape. We cannot see energy and power due to their in capabilities of occupying space. To feel the presence of such powers in our surrounding, we often take the support of our senses and feelings. In some cases our observations are evidence based, in some other cases it may have some imaginary propositions. Here comes the act of limitations that restrict us to feel Ultraviolet and Infrared [2]radiations which remained off the band of the visible spectrum and duly restricted our sense of vision seven visible waves of light.

There arises another question related to our effort of analyzing the relevance of the teachings of The Gita in present day situation. It was the instructions delivered by Lord Krishna to Arjun during the epic age of Vedic Civilisation. That time war had its presence in the scope of royal management. That time conflicts had a final termination to war for making efforts a result oriented. Sins and sinners had their presence in olden times and are still there with us today; format and geo-locations might vary; arms and ammunitions might differ. Even from the pages of history we can see how Prince Ashoka smashed the Kingdom of Kalinga only because that kingdom had refused to hand-over the murderer of his mother to him. Later on the war and the loss of lives of many innocent people had implied a deep impression in his mind and he had decided to refuse to take part in any other battle simply meant for territorial expansion. Teachings of The Gita have worked differently during different instances of the development of conflicts and agony.

Since conflicts and agony are beyond the scope of any historic time line, we can correlate teachings of any instances to prepare a strategic actions of any other present day sectoral management plans. It has the impetus of the absolute knowledge of human actions, wishes, wills and conducts with absolute apprehension of delivering the needful.

The reason of discontentment, sorrow and agony of Arjun after entering the battle field was rejected instantly by Lord Krishna through implying a sanction of his indulgence in the war. Killing any individual or creating another one is not the role of any warrior. A warrior can deliver the duty in time with a clear impetus of making the wiser side victorious. Sinners will lose their lives because of their mis-conducts only.

[1] Hindi term Katha means Stories. Saint Vinoba Bhave translated Shri Madbhagvadgita in Marathi and also wrote a series of books to explain teachings of Gita through simple stories which were also contextually relevant.

[2] Both Ultraviolet and Infrared Radiations are the parts of the invisible band of spectrum incorporated in the Solar Radiation. Our visual sense organ can feel the presence of only visible spectrum comprising seven different colours.

Addressing Aspirations

It is natural that we always consider our own effort a balanced one and a time tested one. All our efforts are basically guided by the skills, competence and capabilities we possess. We rarely consider it necessary to listen to others while planning for any actions. History envisages a fact that actions duly planned without adequate involvement of the aspirations of people in general remained off the side of prosperity and collective progress.

A Balanced Way Out

If we try to learn from our past experiences then the fact becomes clear that China is lagging behind in working out their chances to nullify conflicting situation in Afghanistan. The vacuum might be filled up by the sanctions made to Taliban led government in terms of working out an opportunity of implying a strong hold upon the minerals and other resources they have. They always intend to move forward along with their specific colour of compulsions and desires. Taliban also maintains their adequate alignment with the format of a forceful governance for making people bound to follow set of instructions. Communismic intentions remained active in the country since 1979 onwards. It has got its alignment to imply a hold upon the national politics under the patronage of extremist group of the country.

Oppositions should have adequate presence in governance and judiciary to materialize acts and conducts of all the law enforcement agencies properly. Active ethnic groups such as the Pashtuns, Tajiks, Hazaras and Uzbeks are free to work out a comprehensive plan of prosperity. They also start seeking support of international community for making their stand clear. The voice of people will come in the fore –front efficiently through ballot only. It will be the duly of all the nation states to move on exercising implementation of human right codes through winning the confidence of native Afghans. Superimposing any cultural compulsion may not be an effective way out for solving the conflict. If we bring people close to justice and equality then the chance of the retention of sustainability will be maximised. Our effort should be pro people and with the active involvement of people. If any nation states moves through an armed rebellion then there arises a chance of abusing the situation by certain oppressor class or by certain extrimists. If such class of people are outnumbered by the moderators and liberals then it will be confirmed that law and judicious governance will be established.

Confidence Building

If any community loses confidence upon the government and judiciary then it becomes confirmed that such judiciary or governance may not sustain for a longer time. Situation is more or less same regarding the stand of Afghan youths. They have lost their confidence and faith upon their own judiciary and governance. It was continuing till date due to presence of a foreign force in their land. The system started collapsing instantly just after the exit of such kind of moderating power. Government lost their immediate hold upon the segments of community. Because of this reason armed rebellion outnumbered the potentials of Afghan forces and took the lead.

It is, therefore, becoming confirmed that we must win the confidence of people for making an effort fruitful and result oriented.

Care Management

Once Matsuhita Institute of Government and Management has organized a seminar to publish one of its ambitious management model titled Zero Defect System. It was also popular in American Industry since 1964.[i] The model was really ambitious and also was filled with doubts regarding its applicability. The reason was very simple: Defect can be pointed out in a system by some other individual having some other apprehensions of knowledge. Defectiveness of a system also depends upon the group of people having access to any segment of process, system or operations. A new dimension came in this management model in the form of quality assurance.[ii] An action plan became popular which aimed finally towards became the organizing, motivating, and initiating elements of Zero Defects.

Absolutes of Quality Management model came in practice with a 14 point operational strategy.[iii]

In due course of time four absolutes of Quality Management were identified by Crosby[iv]

These absolutes were as follows:

Quality can be defined according to conformance to requirements.

Prevention is the system of quality.

The zero defects standardise the performance.

Price of nonconformance is the measurement of quality.[v]

Leading Management organizations worked out the relativity of the defectiveness of any system. Some other renowned orgnisations joined hands to work out another management model namely Total Quality Management.

Probably the term "Total Quality" was coined for the first time by the Department of Trade and Industry of United Kingdom during 1983.[vi] It was implemented with certain effectiveness by Defense Department of United States.[vii] It was also pointed out that the increase in quality standards will come through a continuing process of evaluation and refinement of the system implements.

In the model implement of TQM the quality was defined in accord to the requirements of the reference group. The responsibility of maintaining quality was solely considered as the subject of the higher authority engaged in the system implements.[viii]

An attempt to standardize quality parameters was made by Belgium, France, Germany, Turkey, and the United Kingdom. Finally during 1990 all the quality parameters and system implements are finally superseded by ISO 9000.[ix] [x]

Relativity of Quality

Quality itself is a relative term that depends entirely on the quality apprehension of a limited group of people. It often implies subtle variations in between two or more quality concerns of people getting involved in delivering or accepting the services and products from the unit under consideration. What we understand as a best quality can be appreciated with some limitations to some other group of people. They may point out some of the hidden demerits of the product or services as per their level of understanding. It would be more advisable to skip and come out of the standardization of any products or services in terms of any quality parameters. More perpetually to say, one can take care of the entire system on the basis of the level of understanding a person is maintaining. Enhancing the level of knowledge and understanding and implying the same while delivering services will be a cyclic dimension of the Care Management that remain focused upon bringing the best possible services and products from a system implement.

Components one can incorporate in the system of the business cycle, and thematic areas one can keep aside for making the production and processing cycle a cheapest one, are finally reflecting a state of dilemma for any aspirant.

Because of the aforesaid reason and some other quality standards cannot be generalised for all the service and production processes. One cannot apprehend the type, degree and extent of success on the lines of the system implement which might have brought success for some other group of individuals. Development in the refinement process for bringing an absolute standardization in any system in terms of quality is another aspect that led to the exploration of some more perfect management model impregnated with some sort of advanced system implements.

ICT as a Core of the System Implement

These days incorporation of Information and Communication tool in the business cycle is becoming an obligatory affair. ICT is an umbrella term that incorporates a set of communication device in any system implement.[xi] It often speed up the entire process, make the instrumentation process a dynamic one, keep the business cycle at proper pace and allow proper thrust upon the manual involvements. By 2014 the world's capacity to store digital information grew up to 5 zettabytes.[xii] These days nearly 3 billion people register their access to internet.[xiii] It has brought a dramatic change in the communication system through which distantly located stake holders reduced their geographical barriers and registered their presence in desired processes of the efforts related to production and services. Aspects related to Audit and Accounting, regulating human resources, designing process and instrumentation and publishing business related documents are some of the aspects duly covered up through ICT implements. It has even upgraded the entire business cycle through automation of the productivity chain.

Regarding a misconception of replacement of manual work force by the automation, it can be clarified that the entirely automated business cycle will make it more and more result oriented as well as swift and perfectly designed in terms of operational issues. It can even move the process instrumentation towards adequate success mark. Our apprehension with ICT enabled skills of workers getting involved in the entire system will keep the system implements duly involved in the business cycle a vibrant one. It can make the entire system of production and processing a competent one and also it will move up to the globally appreciable standard. The accomplishable quality enhancement may be a gain for some individual or may be meant for the gain of the entire community. Without interacting with other individual, a life process or problems related to the life process may remain un-attended. It may lead toward a chaos due to demand and supply mismatch, due to mismatch in terms of the levels of understanding. A doctor, for instance, may remain unexplored without the approach of fellow patients. Similar the case can be observed in between communications of students and teachers, advocates and clients, shop keepers and customers etc.

Communication is therefore an essential part of human society through which different entities of a system implement often comes closure to each other. It even makes the social and technological functioning appropriate as well as time tested. A farmer can communicate the entity of the immediate requirement for sorting out any problem. Reliance upon mass communication media will ensure a definite progress in time. Communication even brings people together for raising their voice jointly upon any issue. Proper and timely communication even ensures the birth of a vibrant family in the society. Access to information will raise the level of the community consciousness that in turn will increase the levels of the understanding of people. An efficient economic process ensures the total participation of both people and the implementing agencies for enabling the soft and swift confluence of the related services and efforts. Involvement of artisans and workers in a system is primarily determined by the level of experience the referred person is maintaining.

Importance: Service and Individual

We know that works of any individual is recognised in a society on the basis of the importance of the work the person associated with it. Public recognition of any individual in society indicates the importance of the person in society. Doctors and teachers generally receive higher recognition because of the importance of their services. Services of farmers and artisans are equally important in our society because of their involvement in the productivity system. A conscious society can recognize the importance of the members involved in the economy of enterprises. Only conscious members of a family can think about the well beings of a farmer in the society. Such consciousness of people, in turn, will ensure the social security of the members involved in the economy of enterprises. A life process in society, therefore, must not be standardised simply in terms of dress and wealth. It may be standardised properly in terms of efforts and knowledge. Efforts and knowledge are the two important wheels of the collective progress of a society. Standard of living of the rural society may be enhanced by ensuring some of the basic facilities like sanitation, housing, medication, access to education, access to information etc. For enhanced efforts an expanded knowledge base will play a definitive role in making a society developed and sustained one.

Another obstacle that often hampers the normal growth of any Artisan is the insecurity feeling related to the growth and development of certain components having an impact to products and services. Inability of putting forth certain new item in front of the other prevailing ones as an exemplar one often put the effort under question mark. Before placing any item for trial the fellow artisan lose all hope and come to a fixed apprehension for not contemplating upon the effort of making the productivity chain alive. Foremost reason of the sustained insecurity feeling is because of the lack of any financial stability and also lack of their direct regulation upon the market. Marketing professionals usually opt for any item that people become habituated for. They rarely agree upon putting some new item on their tray for a trial. This kind of affinity of the marketing professionals makes the marketing effort a challenging one for artisans. It can be handled properly by adopting some confidence building measures through keeping the artisan in the central focus.

Creating Artisan's group, availing community market network, making all products available at public places, availing market support to artisans by any public enterprises are some of the immediate measures which can enhance the level of confidence of fellow artisans up to a certain extent.

Balance of Demand and Supply

Selection of any product or service for large scale operation is the subject of glancing upon the market for the assessment of the immediate demand of the same. There may be some of the basic questions which can be put forth for such kind of analytical study being conducted by the artisan for the purpose of the product assessment drive. Some of such questions will be as follows:

1. What type of persons gets the immediate benefit of the newly developed product or service?

2. Are there any other sources involved in the delivery of such type of services?

3. If yes, then are there any demerits remain hidden in their products and services?

4. If some demerits of available products and services are duly pointed out, then is the newly launched product and service come up in the market after resolving such demerits?

5. Is there any comparative study on the cost effectiveness of the product and service under consideration?

6. What is the immediate reference area of the product and service that bring out for the business circulation and make the entire stream operational?

7. What are the challenging aspects of the service line up related to making products and services alive?

Thinking upon all sorts of safeguards related to make the effort of productivity a successful one is the aspect that requires immediate attention of the fellow artisan. Keeping oneself aware of the advent of all sorts of difficulties is the immediate requirement of the success indication. Several issues and concerns may remain un- attentive in our way of ascertaining the global trends of peaceful resolutions and conflicts. People maintain different apprehensive thought process for making their associations and immediate concerns justifiable. They even advance their thought process to convince others regarding their stand points of rights and wrongs. It is more conspicuous to nullify the presence of some hidden currents of cross border relations duly inflicted with fulfillment of mutual desires through keeping the immediate surrounding un-attended. Such associations might bring out some worst implications for other global partners ascribed with movement of affinities of across to the same horizon of progress. Some of the nation states may claim that they are sincere enough in addressing issues and concerns related to some common good. The first blotting paper placed on the table of World Health Organisations for justifying their stand point in the context of a global pandemic. It was a serious blow and also invented a furrow in the cemented aspirations of the globally responsive character of WHO. It compelled United States of America to imply a blow upon aspirations of WHO in terms of their exit through the front door of cooperation.

We all are moving towards a society having multiplural characteristics, where people rarely intend to ascribe themselves as a member of any specified group of extremist class in general. They may try to evolve a socialization process having multi-plural characters which will give them a wider scope of internalizing views of different segments of society. They may even start cultivating a work culture amidst a multi-plural and multifaceted human society with a constituent base of humanity and brotherhood. They also start imbibing a globally accustomed cultural base for making them fit enough for the future world order of multi-plural character. We can consider the present day turmoil as an evolutionary ascent through which people started recognising their faiths and beliefs in terms of newly implemented social, economic and religious frameworks. We simply witness the success of a community in imbibing the power of making one fit for the forthcoming days of prosperity.

<u>Care Apprehension for Specially Enabled Ones</u>

A global pandemic might bring some individuals down the track, it may even make a situation challenging for survivors, a terrific situation may be advanced for warriors and even a situation of conflict might bring inmates at the face to face conflicting calamity. The kind of pandemic having no immediate solution can issues a severe challenge for a nation state which might be addressed differently at different war fronts. One such war front is the issues and concerns related to specially enabled persons.

An efficient directives impregnated with a balanced policy framework can ensure the safety of specially enabled persons at work places. It should be adequately addressed alongside the joint consultation of the authorities implementing and monitoring the work place under consideration. It is recommended that an employer who requires a person to undergo any medical, health screening or safety test must bear the costs of the test. If an employee is frequently absent from work for reasons of illness or injury, the employer may consult the employee to assess, if the cause of the illness or injury is a disability that requires accommodation. If practicable, employers should offer alternative work, reduced work or flexible work placement, so that employees are not compelled or encouraged to apply for benefits if they could, with reasonable accommodation, continue in employment. Employers must protect the confidentiality of the information that has been disclosed and must take care to keep records of private information relating to the disability of applicants and employees confidential and separate from general personnel records. At any cost it is not advisable to reject the need of administering medical aid at the tender age in the circumstances of early diagnosis of the biological limitations of the newly introduced individuals having some special capabilities and some clinical or organizational malfunctions. For example differences between anomalies related to Tuberculosis and Leprosy are more or less having identical implications upon the health of the patients. On certain aspects Tuberculosis is more hazardous than compared of Leprosy. But social implications are more in case of Leprosy than compared to Tuberculosis. It is only because Leprosy marks the visible wounds in the form of deformities of limbs and soft body parts. Deformities inside the lungs because of Tuberculosis is not visible, that is why ex patient of tuberculosis gains an easy accommodation in society and a leper struggles a lot to return back to the native family. Deprivations that a leper has to face in society are a common affair in our country. If anyhow some of the medically certified negative patient of Leprosy gains an accommodation in family, that family will be outnumbered and all the family members suffer because of the incorporation of an ex leper in the family. The aforesaid fact raises a question on the acceptability of patient in society and exposure of a patient in society for being exploited. Social safeguards are the subjects awaiting acceptability of people for implementing the same in daily life.

Some sort of escapism prevalent amongst the associates and family members of the specially enabled person make the situation difficult for both the aspirants and aspirers. What are the ways out are matters of our serious concerns. Share and Care Is it true that only parents remain concerned about their ward with some sort of physical or biological limitations?

Can we claim that a state adequately encompasses mechanism for safeguarding the aspirations of specially enabled persons having some specialties and some other limitations? Is there any self-sustained directives and guiding principles through which public service executions gain a sustained confluence of its own kind? Some of the wider dimensions of the enlightened policy standards can perpetuate our query towards attaining the refinement of the state policy standards. The entire job of accommodating people with special capabilities should be shared mutually amongst various active groups of both government as well as voluntary nature.

Some of such initiatives may be of following types:

State should incorporate some of the selected or all of the Enlightened Policy Standards in policy document to be streamlined for the purpose of the state level execution.

Voluntary organisations working in the development sector should design a comprehensive plan document for working out the mechanism of developing a strategy of safeguarding as well as promoting the aspirations of people having special capabilities.

Clinic centers and Health Service Agencies should allocate some of its resources for delivering Social Responsibilities in offering services to people having special capabilities.

Use of appropriate Language is not the only aspect that should be expected from a common citizen, but all such institutions coming in contact with specially enabled people should come across the same lines of principle for designing an ethical stand point of addressing aspirations of people in common.

One should not always point out limitations of the individual, but to encourage the being for the purpose of enhancing skills and competence can make a difference.

Keeping some seats reserved for persons having special capabilities will make them acceptable in society, then also the effort of such reservation is said to be half done without adequate alteration in the sphere of attitudinal interactions in society.

Fundamental human values should be incorporated in the society for making it more vibrant in nature.

Attending the timely need of the people having some limitations may bring some ascribed success of considerable type. They even impart themselves in the regular process of configured activities of special standards. They even make us proud of their stand of imparting themselves in the nation building activities.

None of our living creatures are of any useless type. All the living partners of our society are capable enough in defining their role of percolating their service line ups.

Value addition to the collective progress of any nation in a standardized process can mechanise the entire system in such a way that all the members of that vibrant society become capable of exploring their service profiles in a considerable way. It can even ensure a hundred percent utilization of the human resources that is usually availed to a nation state.

Is Violence the only way out?

Human beings are godly creations with some specialties, and also with some limitations. All individuals are not competent equally in all the fields they tend to aspire for. Success in certain fields of activities and failure in some other fields make all individuals job specific. A teacher can handle the subject in which the excellence is duly attained through some formal training. Considering this context a common affair of the restructuring of skills and competence that an individual ascend with we all plan for certain human development activities and try our best to prepare an individual for the type of statehood or nationhood that one should come up with.

Ascent of the person from a local life to national and further to international life is the subject of capabilities and efforts that one put forth for gaining advancement. All individuals are not experts by born. Skills and competence acquired by them during the period of educational interaction and practices make them special. Fact sheet of disabilities make it clear that we are moving with some sort of limitations by all means. Both quality as well as quantity standards of human development efforts are the matters of concern. There remains some issues and concerns related to development that envisages the need of the refinement of the policy standards to regulate the functioning as well as implementation strategies that required for accommodating the skills and competence possessed by specially enabled person for the collective efforts of national economic progress. How to accommodate such skills and how to move them up through training implements will be the immediate point to be addressed.

Appropriate technologies and selected impairments envisage some of the strategic intervention that makes the human development easier through collaborative efforts of technicians, teachers and other professionals. Leaving any individual in darkness and ignoring the skills and competencies duly housed in that person will be a collective effort assisted with appropriate technologies and assistive standards. Varying impairment standards and their applicability has created a horizon of hope for specially enabled persons through whom they can aspire for implementing their enhanced skills and competence for delivering their duties in more appropriate way. It is the wish factor that often makes a person more active than compared to the level duly estimated while mapping the realms of skills and competence.

Working at The Base

Competency based curriculum design at the elementary level often points out the strength and limitations of a learner at various levels of interaction under various competencies. Such mapping will enable us to move on towards early specialization of the individual having special capabilities. For example, a person with problem of vision may be a good orator.

Not to point out towards the limitations of any individual and to correlate the situation with skills and competence housed in the person will be the highest state of interaction that brings the individual closure to the streams of success. It will even restore the normal functioning of the specially enabled individual aiming towards incorporation of the same entity in the realm of the state level socio-economic and cultural activities. Segmentation of society on the basis of a converged dimension of working capabilities encompasses chances of the formation of close cultural groups having identical job specifications. Such close quarters often acknowledge the presence of their counterpart. Scholars maintained different views regarding addressing aspirations of individuals having enhanced capabilities in certain fields supplemented with limitations of some other degrees and extent.

Question even raised on the necessity of administering medical care if the some physical or physiological malfunctions duly diagnosed at the tender age. In order to implementing an ideal development environment at work places, certain conditions or impairments may not be considered disabilities.

These may include but must not limited to:

Sexual behavior disorders of any kind proved to be against public policy;

Self-imposed body adornments such as tattoos and body piercing etc.;

Compulsive gambling, tendency to steal or light fires; disorders that affect a person's mental or physical state if they are caused by current use of illegal drugs or alcohol, unless the affected person is participating in a recognised programme of treatment duly prescribed by any registered medical professionals or clinics having valid registration of offering such treatments;

Normal deviations in height, weight and strength; and Conventional physical and mental characteristics and common personality traits.

Some of the reasonable accommodation can be of the category of best practices having adequate scope of incorporating skilled individuals for dealing with services and equipment of specific type. There is no general framework of any guideline for focusing the need of people aspiring for a suitable accommodation at service stations or work places, but some exemplar mechanism of such efforts can be placed for explaining the situation efficiently. It may vary in accord to the situation of the place and the nature of interaction with which the service line ups are accustomed with.

Selected examples of reasonable accommodation may be of following combinations by part or by whole:

Adopting existing facilities to make them accessible by specially enabled persons;

 adopting existing equipment or acquiring new equipment including computer hardware and software or some other instrumentations for ensuring the smooth functioning of the individuals with certain limitations of any biological type;

re-organising work stations public places for ensuring safety;

changing training and assessment materials and systems;

restructuring jobs so that non-essential functions are re-assigned;

adjusting working time and leave calendars; providing readers, sign language interpreters, and providing specialised supervision, training and support if needed.

There are certain pre requisites and guiding principles that an employer generally receive from the state executives. Some of the general points to be considered in general may be advanced for strengthening the policy parameters specified for safeguarding the specially enabled employees at work places. When employers recruit they should:

identify the inherent requirements and essential functions of the vacant position; describe clearly the necessary skills and capabilities for the job; set reasonable criteria for selection, preferably in writing, for job applicants for vacant positions. The purpose of the selection process is to assess whether or not an applicant is suitably qualified. This may require a two-stage process if an applicant has a disability: (i) Determining whether an applicant is suitably qualified; (ii) Determining whether a 'suitably qualified applicant' needs any accommodation to be able to perform the inherent requirements or essential functions of the job.

Tests to establish the health of an applicant or employee should be distinguished from tests that assess the ability to perform essential job functions or duties. Health testing should therefore only be carried out after an employer has established that the person is in fact competent to perform the essential job functions or duties and after a job offer has been made. The same applies to medical testing for admission to membership of an employee benefit scheme. [i] Abilities of working with the help of tools and technologies incorporated with Information and Communication Technologies.

There are some other issues which correlates a relationship of employee and employer to which leads the entire system towards a stability in terms of prosperity and vibrant progress.

It should have a definite checklist of system implements through which the evaluation process can be advanced.

Self – Regulating Mechanism

Implementation of any desirable management model from outside without ascertaining the knowledge base of fellow workers can put the entire operation under question mark. It will not ensure the proper regulation of the process in time. Rapid automation of any system implement, for an example, will destabilize the functional vibrations of the group of employee. In some cases they might agitate for the same. System automation was already delayed in countries like India, Pakistan and Bangladesh. It was only because of the lack of digital literacy among people. Some of the socio-political segment of society were also against the automation. Automation was duly accelerated afterwards because of the parallel automation process which went on speedily in countries of Europe and America. It has become an unavoidable wave.

Automation can accelerate the activity of fellow workers getting involved in an co-ordinated operation of system and service. It can also accelerate the entire process of system implement through minimizing information gap and knowledge gap. It will also make the system implement a vibrant one. Service or system check lists of any type will be handled efficiently by the automated system drives. Chances of mistakes will be nullified in some of the system implements. Operational integration of ICT in system, production cycle and services is gaining momentum day by day.

What to Avoid?

There are several things which can be avoided to make the system implement more vibrabt, more result oriented and more secured.

[i] A Guide to Zero Defects: Quality and Reliability Assurance Handbook. Washington, D.C.: Office of the Assistant Secretary of Defense (Manpower Installations and Logistics). 1965. p. 3. OCLC 7188673. 4155.12-H. Retrieved May 29, 2014. Early in 1964 the Assistant Secretary of Defense (Installations and Logistics) invited the attention of the Military Departments and the Defense Supply Agency to the potential of Zero Defects. This gave the program substantial impetus. Since that time Zero Defects has been adopted by numerous industrial and Department of Defense activities.

[ii] Halpin, James F. (1966). Zero Defects: A New Dimension in Quality Assurance. New York City: McGraw-Hill. OCLC 567983091

[iii] Crosby, Philip B. (1979). "8: Quality Improvement Program". Quality Is Free: The Art of Making Quality Certain. New York City: McGraw-Hill. pp. 127–139. ISBN 9780070145122. OCLC 3843884.

[iv] Crosby, Philip B. (1984). Quality Without Tears: The Art of Hassle-free Management. New York City: McGraw-Hill. pp. 58–86. ISBN 9780070145306. OCLC 10277859.

[v] Crosby, Philip B. (1979). Quality Is Free: The Art of Making Quality Certain. New York City: McGraw-Hill. pp.

85–86. ISBN 9780070145122. OCLC 3843884. Quality is free. It's not a gift, but it is free. ... Every penny you don't spend on doing things wrong, over, or instead becomes half a penny right on the bottom line.

[vi] Martínez-Lorente, Angel R.; Dewhurst, Frank; Dale, Barrie G. (1998), "Total Quality Management: Origins and Evolution of the Term", The TQM Magazine, Bingley, United Kingdom: MCB University Publishers Ltd, vol. 10 no. 5, pp. 378–386, CiteSeerX 10.1.1.574.2414, doi:10.1108/09544789810231261, hdl:10317/441

[vii] United States Department of Defense (1989), Total Quality Management: A Guide for Implementation, Springfield, Virginia: National Technical Information Service, OCLC 21238720, DoD 5000.51-G

[viii] Houston, Archester (December 1988), A Total Quality Management Process Improvement Model (PDF), San Diego, California: Navy Personnel Research and Development Center, pp. vii–viii, OCLC 21243646, AD-A202 154, retrieved 2013-10-20

[ix] The ISO 9000 family of quality management systems (QMS) is a set of standards that helps organizations ensure they meet customer and other stakeholder needs within

statutory and regulatory requirements related to a product or service.

[x] Hoyle, David (2007), Quality Management Essentials, Oxford, United Kingdom: Butterworth-Heinemann, p. 200, ISBN 9780750667869, OCLC 72868446, retrieved 2013-10-19

[xi] Kondra, Imaniyal (2020). "Use of IT in Higher Education". UGC Care Journal. India: Studies in Indian Place Names. 40: 280.

[xii] "The World's Technological Capacity to Store, Communicate, and Compute Information", Martin Hilbert and Priscila López (2011), Science, 332(6025), 60-65; see also "free access to the study" and "video animation".

A zettabyte is a multiple of the unit byte that measures digital storage, and it is equivalent to 1,000,000,000,000,000,000,000 [1021] bytes

[xiii] "ITU releases annual global ICT data and ICT Development Index country rankings". www.itu.int. Retrieved 2015-09-01.

Human Aspirations

Human beings have a great advantage in the form of a powerful mind. It is the guiding force depending upon which they make themselves fit for different types of performances in society. They also correlate different events taking place in the nature on the basis of their state of mind and types of knowledge duly acquired by the master of senses. Regulators of all the senses depend entirely on mind for each and every effort. It also correlates the senses and memory to redefine any strategic action in relation of situation and timely need.

Say , for an instance, we cannot sit idle simply by seeing fire in our neighbor's house, because it may invade our houses too. Similarly we cannot say no to any relief and rescue operation during any natural disaster. It may put us in trouble if we remain idle during the moments of emergency. Here lies the exactness of our mind with which it works to correlate situation, timely need and knowledge to cultivate a porper strategy.

Mind is the only place where ideals and ideals generate. Generation of such ideas and ideals directly or indirectly depend upon the knowledge base of a person. Such knowledge base again resides on the segment of skills and competences that a person duly acquired while remaining active during the period of guided learning. The kind of guided learning again depends upon the combination of masterly guides and their adherence towards any culture and tradition. The ultimate root of such culture and tradition in India is the scriptures, Vedas, Upanishads and Brahmans. Some such scriptures and epics are missing due to different reasons. Some other scriptures interpritted differently by different thinkers and in gradual succession people lost their faith on the relevance of such scriptures in modern society. Here lies a mindset with which people work to make things normal and result oriented. We all rely upon our masterly guide with an apprehension of making our presence in the society by remaining active by mind and intellect. The ultimate fate of the learning of such type inflicted with adequate scope of participation helps a learner considerably in establishing a proper balance between the knowledge and intellect.

Gita also helps an individual to understand the exact culmination of the knowledge, senses, skills and intellects with an objective of making the fellow aspirant a vibrant being inflicted perfectly with a sense of performer. Such person cannot escape from the duties, as Arjun was doing; cannot negotiate with sinners; cannot put off weapons amidst a battle field and cannot indulge in conflicts without understanding consequences.

Here one can correlate the state of mind of a doer and the kind of firmness to the duty by considering an incident which took place in a village near Tatanagar (Presently in Jharkhand, India)

Any argument related to existence or non-existence of any supreme power can be addressed suitably through absolute knowledge that we gain in our phases of learning. We have incorporated various aspects related to yoga based life for addressing major aspects of various patterns of manifestations. We also move through limits of our senses for not having capabilities of exploring things beyond the scope of our senses. Simply because of our in-capabilities, for an example, we cannot claim the non-existence of bands of energies like infrared radiation, ultraviolet radiation, magnetic forces, infra sonics and ultrasonic.

An Ascent

Absolute knowledge cannot wait for any material set up to make it evident. It is more confluent than compared to the flow of water, maore faster than the speed of light and more luminous than the strong lumens loke those of stars. It can make people understand things with clear apprehension of putting forth the segment of acts and conducts for the purpose of offering an understanding of facts, figures, events, mechanisms and confluence of information.

Due to lack of such absolute knowledge people often fail to understand the exact reasons behind the manifestation of the supreme power through different living forms. This supreme power resides with identical potential in all the individuals starting from tiny bacteria up to a giant whale. They all combine their own creations with the help of materials present in the real world in an absolute combination of certain format to give a prominent existence. Such individuals can move through the world with certain objectives of leading an assigned life until and unless a band of disintegration of such organic coordination breaks down due to death. In other words, energy is the only super natural power which regulates different components of nature on their way towards creation or destruction of any living form. Absolute knowledge only can make us understand the aspects related to creation and destruction. In Indian philosophy, natural components got the name Prakriti and the super natural component got the name Purush. Communion of Prakriti and Purush makes the creation possible. If such principle is true then it must be evident even at the atomic level of creation; at that level nuclear energy binds the positively charged protons along with some other uncharged particles to make the creation of nucleus possible. Electrons are bound to remain restricted around that empowered core. This mystery of creation signifies the claim of Veda regarding existence of Super Natural Power (BRAHMA)[1] in all the naturally occcoccurringrticles, "Brahma is at all places, within all particles and inside all the beings."

It is the knowledge which becomes visible through various actions of a person. It is that knowledge which differentiates a sage from a begger; it integrates individual apprehensions to materialize each minute actions of that individual for the purpose of defining the final destiny of that person amidst the turmoil of social interactions. That knowledge becomes the guiding force behind senses and guides those senses to assimilate the signals of desired types. Desire is the state of mind which makes the individual apprehension secure within the realm of human actions. It also ensures proper coordination of all the impulses of senses to materialize the desired action. Those guiding force even acts during the process of inter – personal communication. It enables a person to go for accepting or rejecting any communication bands duly offered by some other individual. Differences of such bands of sensual communications can define the enemy and friends from amongst the group of people caome in contact. Distinction of friend and enemy creates a varying matrix of inter-personal communication inflicted with protecting or smashing any individual.

Knowledge increases with corresponding increase in the experiences and mind power. In due course of time mind becomes the store house of all the infmation and avails them to be used by the analytical segment of the brain as per need. Here lies the mystery of success and failure of coordinated senses. It can even define the proper culmination of both the components of the intellect for making the materialization of senses possible. Person with such kind of balanced mind and intellect can speak perfectly, can listen properly, can go for smelling and tasting right things and even can feel the presence of some wealthy impulses in the surrounding.

Any sort of imbalance of mind and intellect can make the senses unfit for materializing any perfect action. The Gita points out the essesnce of attainment of such kind of balances of mind and intellect for regulating senses and making them fit for right and timely actions.

Shopkeepers worship their beloved God before opening the hut, industrious people worship God just before cementing the first brick of their construction works, crafts person worship their instruments during some fixed interval of days to commemorate the supreme power. Worship of energy and efforts is the custom of universal occurrence. There occurs an emotional attachment of artisans with their instruments. They even take care of their instruments on a regular basis. Gradually they come up with an enhanced vision of putting their efforts to keep all the instruments at perfectly operational state. They even consider their instruments as their immediate focus of scheduled daily activities.

Nobody claim the direct interaction with God, but we can feel the presence of such divine power within ourselves. Manifestation of such power will put us at a state of success, where we become fearless in delivering our best possible efforts and services to our immediate reference group. That state of awakening will be the accomplishable goal for any individual including the fellow artisan.

The nature and extent of support, not only in the form of technical knowhow but also in the form of assistance to cope up with market, should be considered for making the system implement appropriate for the rural artisans and farmers. More perpetually one can plan to link up the community with the immediate availability of the resource base for ensuring greater chance of success. Proper combination of Resource, Technology and Skills can define the scope of attaining success. Development workers, since olden times through varying approaches, always worked to search out proper technology, proper mechanism to rely upon, living within minimum, and also moving out of the activities leading toward creation of best possible products and services. They also marked out the fact that technology to be adopted should be people friendly and easy to handle, even it should be compatible to the type of resource base a community relying upon. All sorts of absurdity should be removed.

Lack of confidence upon the system and its implements is the immediate set back that often brings the entire chain of productivity under question mark. One rarely prefers to wait up to the moment of the creation of any enhanced demand of the locally developed products. Better one should launch the implements on an experimental basis duly supplemented with a subtle increase in the productivity.

Financial Institutions always imply a prolonged processing of any appeal of fund. It should be made flexible in terms of availing ease of access to small and marginalised artisans. There is other side responsible for the complexity of the processing of any appeal of finance. Most of aspirants become defaulter while moving across newly implemented enterprise leading toward a severe loss because of the mismatch of resource, technology and knowledge. Yoga based actions never pass on with any blunt apprehension of such failure ultimately leading towards any mis adjustment between resources, skills and technologies. Mis-adjustment of resources, skills and technologies often becomes so worse in some cases that can even put a crafts person or farmer to a life risk. Situation of farmers in Vidarbha because of indebtedness can be placed as an example.

Here we can take an example to exhibit the lack of proper coordination between the planning and implementing agencies duly involved in some development works. One such incident was recorded from the same area of Jharkhand during 1995. Some fellow farmers of Nimdih Block of Saraykela District of Jharkhand received Bullocks financed by a Nationalised Bank. Loss of the life of one of the bullock made another one useless, and in a gradual succession the farmer trapped in the clutch of the financial crisis because of the lack of any immediate return in terms of productivity. The marginalised farmer again trapped in the net of turmoil because of the intervention of a private source of finance for clearing the Bank Loan. The Bank was not in a situation to bring the farmer out of the previous indebtedness because of the rigidity of the financial regulations of the Development Initiatives of the government.

While planning for any industrial activity suitable for a specific rural community, one can imply the credibility of the selected products as per the global standards. Standards of such level can bring the entire system to a stream of implements having more focus upon the look and finish of the outcome to be entangled with the market system. Product should say its own purity and perfectness. It should even attend and apprehend the quality consciousness of people willing to rely upon the same. It should not even break the linkages of demand and supply for enhancing the systematized permanence. This kind of market mechanism will undoubtedly increase the market demand of the selected item.

If any business house of Europe implies stress upon manufacturing Artificial Fabrics with greater success indicators, the same can be housed in the National Economy with higher index of success supplemented with profit. Productivity should go on parallel to the demand that duly created in market. One should remain stick to the mechanism after considering the global demand. Competition alone cannot define any effort as a fruitful and time tested one. One should work to correlate acquired skills and competence of fellow workers with that of the technology available to us. Here arises the need of implementing a discussion on true knowledge.

Veda, Upanishad and other scriptures of Indian origin always describes true knowledge as a subtle confluence of streams of information and skills having adequate power of abolishing the cultural blindness and spiritual rigidness through bringing transformation in characters and will power. Knowledge is the only thing that grows on sharing. It never shrinks to its minimum. A tree of knowledge, as described by saints in Gita, spreads its leaves downwardly in the form of Vedic teachings. The upwardly spreading roots of prosperity receive continuously confluent source of knowledge from the divine and nourishes the entire creation through millions of exhibits of such knowledge. Theory of Relativity, for an example, was not there waiting in the chamber of the fellow scientist. It was there in the cultivation of his skills and ideas which, with an ultimate manifestation, enabled him to link up his observations duly required for deriving the theory. His deeper involvement in that specified faculty enabled him to weave such linkages of theories and propositions.

We always witness the manifestation of such supreme knowledge through its creations. It can even imply a guiding force for all the creature residing in the immediate surroundings. Such a prosperous sacred fig tree (Peepal) can bring forth the absolute knowledge in the form of a normal and continuous confluence of waves of thought processes. Veda described it as an eternal one. It has a sequential expansion having a parallel pace of such considerations through knowledge transformation. Keeping oneself free from illusions and selfishness, one can realise the true nature of absolute knowledge and accordingly can put efforts to gain such knowledge at its absolute nature for making oneself contented and complete.

Down flow of senses and sensible actions become materialised through passage of such waves from the divine to the disciple with an active involvement of masterly minds. This confluence of knowledge and related mechanisms properly explained in chapter fifteen of Gita. One can get rid off the confluence of such relationships of manifestation by cutting the linkages of willingness and desire by using weapons of absolute knowledge. Desires[2] and wishes in the form of leaves grow downwardly growing tree and gains further enrichment through addition of more concepts and propositions by saints. The hidden core of all such knowledge resides only in the absolute confluence of pure knowledge through roots.

If one start moving from leaves and move gradually towards rootlets, then the enlightenment come in the form of repeated crystallization and refinement of knowledge in a regular progression. The final destiny in this way will be

Divine only. Involvement of such power in all sorts of creations and actions become critical at that moment. In actual sense the source and the destiny of the confluence of energy experiences a linkage between various aspects of manifestation. Normal confluence of energy through the cycles of creation and destruction are absolutely inseparable ones. A Black Hole, for example at this critical juncture, is the seat of destruction and creation. From one side all matters and manifestations winded up for accelerating the pace of reversely directed streams and waves of creation.

This absolute knowledge empowers us adequately and facilitates us vividly during our process of identifying presence of divine in every individual with an absolute state of our contentment. Gita even facilitates us in the process of our understanding of the evolutionary trend remaining evident in the biosphere.

We can take the example of the experiences gained by a saint namely Madhavdasji [3]during his wandering days in holy places. The saint was with an absolute state of devotion and used to collect remaining food left out by saintly persons of Ashrams. From such a collection he used to offer it to the Divine first. It was his daily routine activity. One day he was late in moving out for collecting such residues from ashrams and because of forgetfulness he had taken a few without offering it to the Divine. After taking the food in mouth he has realized his mistake and started weeping like a child. He went on weeping in the same posture and the food remained in his mouth.

He was in a dilemma of his inability of taking any concrete step. He cannot take that food without offering it to his lord, even he could not spit it out for insulting saints who had offered him that food. With such a simplicity and contentment he had an experience of feeling the presence of his master within himself only.

Madhavdasji experienced presence of Divine power near him and got an instruction offering the same food that was there in his mouth. Such a call was even firm and absolute for conferring the presence of similar power within himself. It was directing him to forget about physically evident differences. This state of mind developed in Madhavdasji because of his absolute contentment and faith on the source. He has sacrificed all his wishes worries for incorporating the impulse of Divine in the form of absolute impulse of thinking and action. His actions has correlation with mind and intellect and his intellect was developing on the basis of his repeated actions and meditations.

We cannot go blindly driven by the waves and impulses of our senses. There must occur a regulation for quantifying our relations of mind, intellect and sense organs for harnessing a success for us. Here lies the secret of the instructions inscribed in The Gita in the section of the Yoga of Knowledge (Jnan Yoga), where regulation of senses is the first step towards making the mind fit for recognizing the presence of the Divine within the bodily existence. Feeling such omnipresence of the divine is the state of mind which brings renunciation for an individual.

[1] Section 14, Chapter 3, Upanishad:

Sarvam khalvidam brahma, tajjalaniti santa upasita, atha khalu kratumayah puruso yatha-kratur-asmin-loke puruso bhavati tathetah pretya bhavati, sa kratum kurvita.

Meaning: Brahma is the only supreme power. Everything comes from that, sustain in that and finally returns to that, is the only power which empowers us all. People study all the aspects related to what dissolves in that, comes from that and works due to that.

[2] Desire is a state of mind that gives birth to a strong feeling to have something in acquisition or an affinity of wanting something to happen.

For example: I desire only to be left in the state of peaceful mind. Desire cannot kill any intellect, but in a long run, it can suppress the chances of a shift of mind towards something innovative.

[3] Madhavdasji |(1798-1921) was from Bengal and later on entered Vaishnavism. He learned a lot to acquire all sorts of knowledge on Hathayoga duly proposed and framed earlier by Saint Patanjali.

Everlasting Resolutions

Credit goes to saint Patanjali[1] for the development of a most scientifically actualised Yoga conduct meant for the advancement of individual followed by a collateral advancement of the society and of the commune. His proposal is even perpetually designed for accommodating different aspects of a noble life process duly meant for experiencing feelings of collective ascent through the paths of spirituality.

The journey begins with a proposition of following rules of Yama (a set of acts meant for individual purity). It proposes that a person having aspiration of moving through the Octagonal path of Yoga should be nonviolent, truthful, altruistic, self-contented and worshipper of knowledge. While explaining the core philosophy of Nonviolence, the saint proposed the state of mind that considers all the other beings as a family member can claim that the individual is experiencing a true state of nonviolent life.

The second fold in this life comes in the form of some rituals for gaining purity and perfectness of organs and senses. There lies the importance of cleanliness, contentment, self study, sacrifices and worships of the divine. It will simultaneously purify both the mind and body for making the individual and the referred community fit for the ascent up to the third state of this Yoga conduct.

Third stage is meant primarily for balancing the body, mind and intellect through positioning oneself in some proposed postures, termed popularly in Indian Philosophy as Asana, and regularising the same through day to day routine works. While describing such positioning, the saint says that the kind of position which offers a stability of mind, body and intellect is the Asana in its true sense. Whatever may be the posture and whatever may be the name for such posture, true Asana can only bring desired stability of mind and body.

Fourth stage of the Ascent is vital one because of its involvement in diverting senses towards the inner conscious mind through regulation of the breathing and confluence of senses through specified neural transmission. The core philosophy ascribes the establishment of a hold on the breathing and bringing it down at least below 15 per minute. It is also designed for channelizing the breathing through different nerve channels for infusing senses in the deep conscious mind for making it awakened and contented. This process is most vital one because of its importance in making the individual capable of diverting senses towards the inner world for roaming around the acquired knowledge and rearranging such acquisitions by repeatedly meditating on them. It can be also described as a process of self actualisation and self contentment. Such contentment only can enable a person to move through the inner world of senses and knowledge. It can be more confluent because of its mild infiltration through all the senses. It can make a person see what the mind wants to see, it can listen in accord to the inner sense, and even taste, smell and touch things accordingly.

Development of positive waves in mind because of the prolonged meditation, the individual makes oneself fit for experiencing the practice of withdrawal from the external world for enabling oneself perpetually confined upon the attained knowledge and quantify oneself for further attainment of true knowledge. Such a withdrawal (PRATYAHARA) makes the person competent for making oneself refined and more perpetual for the ascent of the soul a step ahead for the attainment of a feeling related to the presence of the divine in the life process. It can even imply a guiding force for the individual duly required for rearranging the absolute knowledge for the purpose of making it more vibrant, more confluent and more actualised.

All the five stage practice brings a state of enlightenment for the individual and make the person fit for feeling the true meaning of life, real goal of life and all sorts of lively involvements in the community and society , in a broader sense, in the universe. Such an actualisation (DHARANA) makes the person fir for meditating upon the stand point repeatedly with an aspiration of bringing refinement. Movement and journey of any person through this stage depends entirely upon the degree and expansion of the knowledge duly acquired by the person in life. It can ascertain the attainment of such a state of mind at the stage where senses, memory and intellect culminate perpetually with an apprehension of spiritual ascent.

Sensual, intellectual, spiritual and social convergence mounted voluntarily in an individual brings a state where the conscious mind intends to meditate repeatedly. This state of Concentration (DHYANA) enables a person to feel the presence of such a divine power in so many different states of individual and different life forms of all types moving around in nature. Their purpose of survival, their inter dependence and other hidden mysteries start becoming clear during concentrating upon the related process and propositions. A warrior, for example, can concentrate properly at the specified target. Such a perpetual concentration can bring further refinement in senses, memory and intellect with an objective of making them more actualised, more contented and more balanced.

Fixing mind, intellect and senses upon the true attainable goal in life is the final stage (SMADHI) where the person can feel the presence of Divine in the centrally actualised memory, intellect and senses. It will become a guiding force for the individual and make the person competent for gaining spiritual advancement in life. It will even make the life a meaningful and perpetually contented. It is the desired stage of life where person aspires to ascend through practices, acts and conducts. At all instances it is not necessary that all people should move through all the eight folds of Yoga. The state of mental and spiritual contentment or a state of saturation aspiring for mental stability will exhibit the advent of Samadhi.

We cannot claim that individuals imparting oneself in society for delivering services or for playing some other definite role are perfect by all means. They work ceaselessly in due course of time for attaining perfectness in a gradual succession. Some people may consider an individual as perfect as compared to some other. One player may be considered a best one in his or her team. In gradual succession best ones will be identified through tournaments and some other best ones may be compared globally to select the globally best one. But, what about that skilful player who had decided not to take part in any tournament? The kind of act exhibits the limitation of the evaluation process as a whole.

The comparative process of examining and assessing perfectness parameter is standing on the basis of certain directives usually made by a group of people. Because of that reason any perfectness parameter cannot claim that individuals moving through the screening of the perfectness examinations are absolutely perfect. We can work put billions of questions from any specific field of study. Moving through such a massive task might make the life of any aspirant a hell. The type of testing in the form of written interaction is usually made limited by incorporating a set of planned interactions and content areas with a pre – planned format of study.

We cannot claim that our all acts and conducts are perfect. We can simply claim that we all try our best to attain completeness in our life through making our lives more and more actualised through processes, as we feel, fit for us. It will bring a kind of perfectness. The claim of any individual regarding the state of perfectness depends upon the state of knowledge that the person gained through practices. Perfectness of one individual from any specified viewpoint might be of different type as per the understanding of some other individual. Such a difference in terms of observation and actualisation makes the term perfectness a relative one.

With relative consensus perfectness can be of relatively advanced one or may be of degraded one. That is why we feel that all individuals should have an apprehension of refining oneself repeatedly keeping pace with refinements and actualisations in the field of knowledge acquisition.

A management school of Japan once started claiming that the management model duly designed and implemented by them is a model residing on the Zero Defect System. In due course of time that management model was replaced by the term Quality. The name coined for that management system was Total Quality Management. With further experiencing and related experimentations people came to know about the fact that the term Quality is a relative one. It has no correlation with the absolute sense of any management. Upgraded qualities of any type might have some degraded apprehensions from some other view point. That is why quality is considered as a relative term. Further advancement and actualisation in the process orientation related to operation management gave birth to a more meaningful model of management termed Total Care Management. The term Care can be actualised as per the level of knowledge and can be refined repeatedly as per need. This management model remained sustained in the community level activities of varying types.

We consider the God as a perfect one and we also aspire for gaining such perfectness with a set up of our mind for having an opportunity of feeling the presence of such completeness in our mind , intellect and senses. It will make our life meaningful through bringing actualisation of the self. It will also make us more contented through adhering all our efforts of culminating actions and propositions for a common good.

The act of Sabari [2] , as described by saints in the Ramayana, was a perfect one. The process of conducting a leading warfare against the Demon King by Lord Rama was also a perfect one. The eleven qualities duly exhibited by Lord Shiva and identified accordingly by Goddess Parvati were also perfect ones. They have decided to set an example through generating a legendary character, namely Hanumana (the wise monkey), for exhibiting the true culmination of Knowledge and Devotion with an objective of bringing success in all actions. Success of Hanumana was also residing in the fact of proper culmination of Knoweledge and Devotion.

Here we came, with an ease of access and understanding, at the last segment of discussion about essence of karma Yoga in life through maintaining a faith on the philosophical doctrines re-established in society through proposals of Gita. It was witenssing the junction of dual battles that the person was fighting just after entering the battle field. The Yoga of sorrow and discontentment as exhibited by Arjun in The Gita was the juncture where the person had to become victorious upon some inwardly active enemies. Anger, ego, discontentment, fear and some other similar enemies may put a person in trouble during the stage of a standpoint where the person has to fulfil all his duties, acts and conducts through exhibits of will power and courage.

Yoga of Knowledge and Action, as described with some proposed practices in Gita, always intend to bring absolute coordination between actions and intellect for making efforts a successful one. It is also proposed that the person should move on further to perform duties without wasting time by waiting for any desired results of actions to come. Such kind of adherence, meant towards the result of any action, may distract the effort of any individual and make the effort a partially accomplishable one.

Perfectness by all means may remain in nature, may equip a person in different ways and may configure the efforts with more prominent results. It may even make people aware by different means of progress. If one aspires individually about attainment of progress by keeping aside aspirations of other fellow partners of society, then we can say that such aspiration may never bring a reality because of the prevalence of linkages and cross linkage remaining evident in society.

Veda speaks about presence of such perfectness in God and aspires for cultivating the same by any individual through repeated and regularised practices of Yoga and Meditation.

We may continue discussion further more upon the same topic for making the fact about essence of Yoga in life a clear and prominent one. We can even represent hundreds and thousands of more examples to highlight the essence of Yoga based life process as an ideal one. On the basis of such fact it is advanced that the effort will continue in future with an aspiration of bringing more live experiences for establishing the role of Yoga based life process in making society a vibrant one.

If we aspire for our own progress, with incorporating the necessity of the progress of other, then we must move on through materialising ambitious projects for ensuring progress of all the other individuals. Progress of such type with a collective apprehension will bring success by all means. It will also make the entire community a vibrant one. People living in a community are interlinked at various instances. In a natural way we cannot sanction access to different types of water and different types of air for respective members of the community simply on the basis of their socio-economic standards.

People should enjoy their access to resources with an easiness for ensuring their active participation in the socialisation process of the entire group. Any implements or plans meant for a specific community should have all other parameters duly required to minimise the communication gap, information gap and cultural gap which often become the root cause of some community level tensions.

Philosophy of Karma Yoga alongside the integral approaches will become the central force during consideration of any implements having scope of Progress of all the members of society.

Participation, simply meant for keeping people in confidence, while implementing any development activities, may not bring fretful result. It should have adequate scope for accommodating ambitions and wishes of maximum number of people in any planned development initiatives and work plans. One can grant a sanction upon any plan or one may directly oppose the stand of community leaders. Development workers remaining involved in the planned actions should have adequate explanations for gaining the confidence of people at all the levels of society.

Ignorance of any of the community member will turn into socially developed wounds in the form of a shadow area of information and communication. Such shadow area will become the birth place of anger, hatred, tension and communal violence. There are examples in which we can see the people of oppressed classes become violent and start planning differently for exercising their rights.

If any legal and judiciary system loses confidence of people then there are chances of violations of such law at the respective level of community in which people lost their faith on the judiciary. Flexibility of the judiciary should ensure the scope of implementing any exercises for regaining confidence of people on the judiciary.

People impart in the socialised system in which they feel themselves adequately protected and properly internalised. Their rights should have adequate social and legal safeguarding. Without gaining the confidence of people we cannot expect them to cater their duties towards the society perfectly. Bhagat Singh worked and sacrificed for the freedom of India in one hand and agitated differently against British on the other. Britishers wanted to smash him by putting him in the dark room and finally by sentencing him till death. Community of Indian origin started working out a strategy of violating the state law for making their leader free from the clutch of oppressors. In this way one person may simultaneously gain the status of mind to differentiate some friendly community and enemy. People may finalise their stand about any community on the basis of their predetermined ambitions, wishes and willingness.

The State of Knowledge Confluence

There exists different literary and ritual sources having enough potential to correlate the human practices and related philosophical beliefs. We cannot simply deny the existence of any supreme power only on the ground of its non-visibility. In some cases such supreme power may remain off the limit of our senses. If we try to sum up all such teachings duly proposed by thinkers and philosophers of olden times, then the collected instructions will become enriched one. It will address all sorts of propositions and concern related to various aspects of our daily life.

Most interpreted literature among all is Bhagvadgita. Different saints considered it differently and also tried to work out its relevance in our daily life. Relevance of the teachings of Gita has an everlasting impression in the minds of thinkers and philosophers.

Most commonly discussed part of all such propositions is the considerations related to the essence of Karma Yoga (the Yoga of Performance, Actions and Perfections). We cannot translate the Sanskrit term "Karma" directly as

"Actions" in English. The term Karma has a wide range of considerations. It correlates skill acquisition, mental preparedness for getting indulge in activities, establishment of correlations in between different aspects of life and remaning attached to the aspects of actions and perfections.

It is also true that we cannot segregate any living being from its external world. We can even assign a definite task for that individual on the basis of the skills and competence possessed by the same. Our expectation from that individual will be centralised on the basis of such considerations. We consider that individual successful only after ascertaining the meaningful and fruitful participation of the same in the proposed action. A knowledge base empowers an individual to define its role in society, or to work in the extended environment. It can even ascertain its own horizon of activities. That individual can even surpass trying days with the help of the organised framework of knowledge.

We acquire skills in life through series of interactions and training, gain competence through guided practices, confine ourselves to certain segments of duties and concerns as per wishes, mechanise our welfare and warfare for fulfilling individual as well as collective concerns and claim our status on the basis of our role in the community. Through all such efforts, carrying types of skill acquisition and knowledge confluence, we feel the presence of a masterly power having affinity of guiding the self. It even intends to make an individual a special one by providing scope of ascent in terms of spirituality. Spirituality of specific type and its expansion by all means is the subject where mind, body, skills and competence culminate properly to ascertain the refinement of an individual.

While talking about absolute knowledge with its super confluous characters we may feel some sort of difficulties due to limitations of our senses. We want to see some relevant things, but our senses may not equip us properly in doing so, similar the situation is regarding all other senses. Such kinds of sensuous limitations compelled us to imagine about the presence and propagation of some super natural things with extra ordinary characters. We cannot segregate matter and energy in our surrounding by any means or by any mechanism. Energy involvement is there even at the stage of certain sub atomic state of bindings. In the same way we cannot segregate the God or divine power from its creation. We can feel its presence but may not be able to describe it by furnishing evidences. We can talk upon it the way a blind person talks to another visually impaired ones, or like a physically challenged one with another person having similar limitations.

Our present effort is a continuation of all such previously organised efforts of making the divine confluous through our senses, making an individual feel its presence within the sub conscious mind. An earthen candle cannot describe its glory. It is the subject of other individuals having an opportunity of getting enlightened amidst darkness by placing oneself juxtaposed to the earthen candle with an affinity of getting illuminated. The Sun cannot describe itself by any means, it is solar radiation and the act of Nuclear Reaction taking place at the surface of the sun which describes the power game of the ignited giant. We also cannot put us in a move to reach the surface of any star to examine the mechanism duly involved in its affinity towards act of availing radiations, we can feel it and gain it with its graceful vitality to enrich ourselves.

There are many other instances available in our nature that describes vividly the presence of such divine power with its empowered vigil of creations and destructions. We can simply feel them, and in certain instances correlate them with our acts of creations and destructions. We can even make some of our efforts a prolonged one through designing participatory efforts of specific type for enlightening the phenomenon of the divine omnipresence. It is the realm where all individuals in this planet can feel the essence of exercising the global communion and can impart themselves in making the nature more confluous, more vibrant, more and more habitable and more prosperous.

Spirituality brings lives closure, makes people awakened, provides a scope of feeling the presence of divine power within the scope of living beings and intensifies our senses and makes us more contented for gaining the power of our effort of assimilating knowledge.

In this publication we limit our discussion on and around the relevance of Karma Yoga in present day context. Yoga of Action, Perfectness and Performance has a close link up with the knowledge base of a performer, because of that reason we can point out some aspects of the confluence of knowledge to enlighten the core principle of Yoga in an integrated fashion. It will be more exemplar for people to ensure its practical utility. Things already mentioned in Upanishadas were pitched in again in Madbhagvadgita to make people aware of the practical utility of acts and conducts of a Yoga based life.

A Yoga based life can have a sense of completeness for ensuring complete unfoldment of petals of skills and competences. It will even make people aware of the ongoing situation. Because of that reason also Yoga comes in the fore front of discussion time to time with a clear apprehension of individual as well as collective progress.

Our tendency to add a prefix with the term Yoga by using different terms like Karma(action, perfection, skills and competence), Jnan(knowledge), etc. All such ideals related to Yoga ultimately points out towards the accumulation of some positive waves for experiencing a link with the Divine and, at some higher states of practice, to feel the presence of such Divine in every creation. When any confluence of such positive waves come on surface through experiences and practices we cannot bifurcate them from one another. It is also a state of feeling the presence of all such waves with a band of stress on some other states of Yoga. Confluence of action, perfection or skill, for an example, without adequate support of knowledge may not be a desired result of Yoga. Here becomes the concept of Integral Yoga alive.

Any individual having an aspiration of gaining ascent in life through developing an understanding on the principles of Integral Yoga can go through it repeatedly. One time reading may be an eye opener. Language of this work is kept simple to enable a person having some basic knowledge of the language can explore the entire representation in original.

Students learning in high schools can also use it as their reference manual for developing their own understanding on the Philosophy of Yoga and Meditation. It can successfully enable them to develop their own ideas on the practical aspects of Yoga and Meditation.

Whenever we interact on yoga, a commonly discussed name usually comes in our mind, Saint Patanjali, the creator of eight fold Yoga Philosophy (Ashtanga Yoga). It has a long lasting impression on the lives of people moving across it by part or by full. It is the path through which one can purify one's mind, body and intellect. People having affinity towards Patanjali and his principles of yoga can also go through this book to ascertain oneself in the real world situation.

This yoga philosophy is also helpful for individuals having an affinity towards attainment of true knowledge which is required for reallocating the skills, competence and intellect in one's mind to facilitate proper manifestation of the individual within stipulated time frame of the cycle of life.

Any argument related to existence or non-existence of any supreme power can be addressed suitably through absolute knowledge that we gain in our phases of learning. We have incorporated various aspects related to yoga based life for addressing major aspects of various life forms. We also move through limits of our senses for not having capabilities of exploring things beyond the scope of our senses. Siply because of our in-capabilities, for an example, we cannot claim the non-existence of bands of energies like infra red radiation, ultraviolet radiation, magnetic forces, infra sonics and ultrasonics.

Learning even continued beyond the scope of interactive curriculum transaction with an aspirations of enhancing critical skills and confidence of the active members of the society.

In simple words, we can say that the advanced Value system enabled people to understand and maintain their fundamental value system on the basis of the popular cultural and traditional base of olden times. For widening this type of practice with an aspiration of collective progress, people started sharing minute particulars of their feelings on any specified thing or propositions to keep the progressive trend active and to ascertain its ascending mode.

The gradual refinement in value system has come in the form of rituals and observations. In modern day context the human value system has a character of an exhibit of a convergence of differently developed value systems. The kind of convergence of both eastern and the western value system has enabled the development of Missionary Culture in the Indian context. Such missionary culture has enabled people to readjust their acts and conducts on the basis of some masterly instructions that they duly received through scheduled discourses of their masterly guide. None of such value system is entirely aligned towards the west and not even towards the Vedic culture. Combination and recombination of value system always reflect some sort of Yoga Philosophy with an affinity towards naming it differently for making oneself satisfied. Lord Buddha, for a simple example, has cultivated eight fold simple path of worship having a proposition identical to that of the Yoga Philosophy and acts and conducts duly proposed by Saint Patanjali. The path proposed by Lord Buddha became popular in some of the society due to advent of easiness in the worship.

The missionary culture in Bengal duly introduced by Shri Ramakrishna has the identical affinity of bringing the Yoga based acts and conducts to people with easiness. It has also designed a service oriented mechanism of worship based on the principle of "Serving Man, Serving the Divine." It has also gained success and brought its prominence through cultivating ideals of Saint Patanjali. Ramakrishna wanted people to keep faith on the presence of the Divine. As we cannot feel the presence of all kinds of waves of energy because of our limitations of senses, similarly we cannot feel the omnipresence of the supreme power within us because of our in-capabilities of imbibing the waves of the supreme power. Only because of this reason we cannot deny the presence of such divine power within ourselves and within the others.

We can see things as they occupy a definite shape. We cannot see energy and power due to their in capabilities of occupying space. To feel the presence of such powers in our surrounding, we often take the support of our senses and feelings. In some cases our observations are evidence based, in some other cases it may have some imaginary propositions. Here comes the act of limitations that restrict us to feel Ultraviolet and Infrared radiations which remained off the band of the visible spectrum and duly restricted our sense of vision seven visible waves of light.

Once people of Kolkata wanted to judge the knowledge base of Saint Ramakrishna. A group of learned persons and veterans from the city visited the temple where Ramakrishna used to deliver his services by preying goddess Kali in his own language and also by claiming incidents of his conversation with Goddess Kali. The matter became very critical when Raasmani, the main patron of Ramakrishna, came to know about this incident. Inmates of the temple and the royal family wanted to work out any alternatives, but firmness of Ramakrishna made them more confident about the knowledge enrichment that the saint had.

People came in and took their respective seats within the small residential block of the fellow saint. His happiness and contentment exhibited his firmness and fearlessness. People prepared to throw questions towards him. With a gentle smile Ramakrishna described a narration in short, "Once an idol made of salt moved on to measure the depth and expansion of ocean. We all can easily imagine what happened to that idol. Returning back from his status became impossible. I have nothing more to say, now it's your turn. Ask me."

The kind of voice and firmness to face all sorts of questions made people worries about their own limit of knowledge. Ramakrishna had narrated an incident which was from Vedantic teachings. It made people confirmed about the knowledge enrichment of the saintly person having a common look with some uncommon adherence to the immediate divine. The judgement went on differently and some among them had accepted

Ramakrishna as their true guide in their respective path of spiritual ascent.

Spirituality, in its true sense, should not put any individual off the track of society and culture. It should cultivate the essence of true knowledge for the purpose of the collective enrichment of the referred commune through making their overall spiritual ascent towards integral progress more and more confluous.

Instead of having all such knowledge of Veda, Epics and other spiritual worshipping mechanism, Ramakrishna preferred offering food to Goddess Kali in the way people offer to any other living beings. The kind of contentment itself exhibited his effort of linking people of some common living to their holy mother and immediate divine.

Depth and expansion of the knowledge is so enormous that we can simply feel it and try to acquire it by part on the basis of our capabilities, willingness and interests. Once people of Kolkata wanted to judge the knowledge base of Saint Ramakrishna. A group of learned persons and veterans from the city visited the temple where Ramakrishna used to deliver his services by preying goddess Kali in his own language and also by claiming incidents of his conversation with Goddess Kali. The matter became very critical when Rani Raasmani, the main patron of Ramakrishna, came to know about this incident. Inmates of the temple and the royal family wanted to work out any alternatives, but firmness of Ramakrishna made them more confident about the knowledge enrichment that the saint had.

People came in and took their respective seats within the small residential block of the fellow saint. His happiness and contentment exhibited his firmness and fearlessness. People prepared to throw questions towards him. With a gentle smile Ramakrishna described a narration in short, "Once an idol made of salt moved on to measure the depth and expansion of ocean. We all can easily imagine what happened to that idol! Returning back to his original status became impossible. I have nothing more to say, now it's your turn. Ask me whatever you want to ask."

The kind of voice and firmness to face all sorts of questions made people worries about their own limit of knowledge. Ramakrishna had narrated an incident which was from Vedantic teachings. It made people confirmed about the knowledge enrichment of the saintly person having a common look with some uncommon adherence to the immediate divine. The judgement went on differently and some among them had accepted Ramakrishna as their true guide in their respective path of spiritual ascent.

Spirituality, in its true sense, should not put any individual off the track of society and culture. It should cultivate the essence of true knowledge for the purpose of the collective enrichment of the referred commune through making their overall spiritual ascent towards integral progress more and more confluous.

Instead of having all such knowledge of Veda, Epics and other spiritual worshipping mechanism, Ramakrishna preferred offering food to Goddess Kali in the way people offer to any other living beings. The kind of contentment itself exhibited his effort of linking people of some common living to their holy mother and immediate divine.

[1] . Saint Patanjali was from the Vedic Civilisation who proposed the balanced life process through pracxtiicng Ashtanga Yoga (Eight fold Yoga) in a regular succession for gaining the enlightenment of oneself and for identifying the Aim in life.

[2] . Sabari was a Tribal Woman who offered fruits to Rama and LAxmana during their progression through the forest. She wanted to know about different types of devotion that a follower can follow through for individual ascent in the path of daily life.

Intellectual Rectification

We are discussing at present about saints like Veda Vyasa, Maharshi Patanjali, Valmiki and many more. Their presence can be ascertained even today through their creations, acts and conducts. They had created a best possible thought process and expected people to imbibe the same for ensuring aspirations of the advancement of the society through rectifications of the individual conducts.

Rectification of such type is a continuous process. We may not be able to claim about the absolute clarity on the process of rectification as an error free system. Such kinds of thought process will remain in the atmosphere even after thousands of years for making people acquainted with such principles.

The kind of thought process will remain in the context in the form of waves. Now a day's wave theory of the propagation of energy from its origin to the seat of action has become a common point of discussion. Wave theory of the propagation of energy form place to place addresses the need of people well in advance.

Thinking and attitude of people coming out from more or less identical socio-cultural background often exhibit similarities of many types. If countries from different socio-cultural background share parts of their border then it will be obvious that they often get indulge in some locally pitched conflicts. We can take the examples of the conflict between Armenia and Azar Bizan. Some other countries also put themselves in with certain vested interests. Communities fighting with each other are not justifiable at any cost. There exists other means of communication through which people move on to express their anger and also they can imply a sanction through business confluences.

Here comes the question of work culture and sectoral coordination. We have also witnessed the attitudinal difference between Rama and Ravana, as vividly described at difference instances in the famous epic the Ramayana. Rama wanted Ravana to give Sita, his life partner, back. He had deputed his messenger twice for making Ravana, the demon king from Sri Lanka, agree upon the proposal of peace.

The proposal of peace was rejected in one hand and the power, potential and courage of lord Rama was ignored on the other. The result came in the form of a war. That war was also not meant for killing all the people of that country. It was not even meant for smashing the kingdom for grabbing resources, nor even meant for putting the name and reverence of lord Rama in the fore front. It was meant for teaching a lesson to the demon king and also for diffusing his state of ego, compulsion and desires.

The thought process that started moving along with the advancement of lord Rama was perfectly captured and imbibed by the brother of the demon king namely Bibhishan. He had managed himself to come out of the darkness of ego, compulsion and desires by harnessing the philosophy of peace, prosperity and collective progress. The result with him was also quite fruitful. He was the victorious person of that battle and duly accepted the place of his elder brother.

The Ramayana, The Mahabharata and other such scriptures always display the victory of good forces over the evil ones through inculcating waves of peace, prosperity, brotherhood, collective progress and prosperity for all. These acts also intensified at some places by linking up the bands of true and absolute knowledge with devotion to bring forth the powers of right action.

Hanumana, the warrior of lord Rama as described in the Ramayana, is the best example of such character having perfect combination of Knowledge and devotion. Once a situation developed in the middle of the journey of the envoy of Lord Rama during the moment when they had to cross a long stretch of ocean to reach Sri Lanka for obtaining information about Sita. All fellows present in the envoy started guessing about their own potential, only the person silent was Hanumana. His seniors wanted to know the exact reason of his silence. Hanumana said that the power possessed by him is obviously enormous, but it is not in his hand. A divine force guides the manifestation of that power. It will be implemented even at the service of the divine. Such knowledge was the exhibit of the true knowledge. Based on that knowledge one can surpass all possible obstacle whichever might come on the way. Similar thing happened with Hanumana. By crossing all the obstacles he reached the destiny and traced out Sita.

Sita noticed the presence of the messenger deputed by lord Rama. Here came the situation where Hanumana exhibited his devotion. For gaining the confidence of Sita on warriors and associates of Rama he had exhibited his enormous power in that garden where Sita was kept under observation. He even wanted to bring Sita back to Rama immediately. He was stopped by Sita by instructing him not to violate the rule of the family and tradition from which Ram is taking the lead. He was requested to follow the assignment in particular for which Rama deputed him.

Here both Sita and Hanumana exhibited their devotion to their immediate master. It was also an exhibit of their loyalty to their master. Such loyalty often culminates to give birth to enormous power with which lord Rama along with his entire envoy was advancing towards the Demon King to teach him a lesson.

The fact was developing beyond the imagination that is why it was not perceivable by persons having inflictions of ego, anger, hatred, self-centrelines and desires. Ravana perceived the development in the envoy of Rama and his advancement towards his kingdom as an impossible task. After noticing the presence of Hanumana in front of him he was not convinced by the powers of monkeys and other associates who were accompanying lord Rama. The waves of devotion of the godly presence, whom Ravana used to worship regularly, continued radiating out through the acts, conducts and attitudes of Hanumana. Then also Ravana was not in a position to accept any chance of the advancement of lord Rama towards his territory. Such standpoint of a warrior develops from the over confidence of the person about the system, implements and parts of such implements.

That over-confidences removes all possible chances of rectification of the system. Because of that reason also Ravana failed to rectify his mistakes and placed himself in the turmoil of trouble.

Whatever lessons we learn from experiences and interactions will sustain in our life for a longer time period. It can even bring sustaining happiness and contentment within us. Here lies the way in which any thought process perpetually moved from one individual to the other.

In the modern world we have various types of cultural and religious thought process possessing rituals, customs and traditions of different types , which are equally competent to enrich people in terms of knowledge, devotion, courage, will power and dedication. The way we receive each culture to enrich our multiplurality will specify our degrees and ranges of success. Our motive force will guide accordingly to explore possibilities of working out converged cultural segments from all the rituals to move up towards vibrant waves of multi plurality.

India , at this juncture of the development of multiplurality, will be a best example for all of us. Here people learned a lot to live with each other, tolerate each other and enrich each other differently.

We cannot see light. Even we cannot see the propagation of sound through the material medium. Light strikes our eye, reaches our brain and develops a sensation of vision through certain life process of vision. With some sort of illusion, or lack of true knowledge only, we often claim that we can see light. Even all the colours radiated out from the sun are not recognisable by us. If God resides inside the individual, if all mysteries related to the ascent of a person on the path of divinity, then why any devotee search it out for gaining the blessings of any Divine power located outside the physically existing body? Why such a dwindling situation any individual face during the tenure of worship?

Lord Krishna narrated essence of feeling the Divine communion with the physically existing life through witnessing cultivation of knowledge, actualisation of the presence of any supreme power in sub conscious mind and possible ways and means to follow that power. It enables an individual to come across the feeling of the advent of some completeness in the mind through knowledge transformation. Cultivation of knowledge regarding the relationship of the divine and disciple is enrouted from the age old traditions through the turmoil of the organic evolution. That evolution brought some change in the process of exhibits, but the core remained the same. It was even more perpetual and more profound regarding the ability of harnessing the relationship of matter and energy. We cannot imagine the existence of matter without the involvement of energy, and similarly energy takes a definite visible form to occupy certain space in this universe.

How do people see things and how do they correlate such unavoidable relationship of energy and matter is depend upon the level of understanding that one adheres with. A master of Physics and a master of Philosophy must have varying degree of explanations for putting forth the mystery behind the mechanism involved during inter-conversion of matter and energy. All organic combinations have certain physical and chemical sets of combinations in such a definite ways that they inculcate the abilities of interactions and abilities of giving birth to senses. Even evolution of sensory structures and related orientations became much collaborative in case of human beings. Here occurs a change which brought us near the state of explorations meant for examining the hidden mysteries behind creation and orientation of life forms in the living planet.

These days, things are known to us that earth like situation exists in the universe. Only the matter of concern is that we may not be able to reach the place even after attaining the speed as that of light in a year or two. Only we can admire the presence and orientation of such creations within our visibility. Only we can explore and examine such things with the help of optical and electronic instruments. With an understanding of such limitations human beings never arranged any voyage to explore the inner world of senses that can allow us to explore the outer orientation of time and space. Such an inner world exploration may require a little effort to culminate senses within a confinement for feeling the presence. There also resides a tremendous flux of energy accumulated within such a small space. Those mysterious combinations taking the form of life were explored differently by saints during olden times.

There developed a science of explorations of the correlations of the Creation and the Divine. Matter and energy indulged in a perfect orientation for letting senses flow through them. Arrangement and orientation of all our senses are directed outwardly. That is why we are bound to receive waves and sparks from the outside world. Our inner world remains unexplored in most of the cases. Only adherence of true knowledge and the journey of senses through inner world during meditation can pave a way out for exploring our own self. Meditation is the doorstep where orientation of senses get diverted towards the inner world and bring out mysteries associated to the fact of accommodation of the Divine power inside the living being.

Is that Divine power is restricted to the human beings only? The answer is, obviously and surely without any doubt, No. human beings has gained some sort of evolutionary supremacy in due course of time, but other beings are also of same potential and courage with a domination of animism in them. Dogs are loyal to their master, cats exhibit better vigilance power, elephants are more socialised beings having better memory power and tigers are the masters of their own territory. Taking hold upon the surrounding and defining the role according to trophic [1] level, we can easily arrange these beings and others without any difficulty.

Philosophical and Spiritual supremacy is a step forward that makes a distinction between other animals and human beings. Then also we can witness inhuman acts from human beings and humanly acts from some inhuman animals. The orientation of sense organ and correlation of senses and sensory responses with memory and intellect is the only factor regulating such varying degrees and conducts of animismic and hunmanismic behaviours.

Presence of such a Divine power within the creation is the reason behind the maintenance of an idea of serving humanity with a correlated apprehension of serving God. Only God cannot put a direct access to the feelings of the presence of such immense power within us. It is the approach with which we offer our services to living beings can develop a way out for us to feel the difference.

Once during pre-independent period in Bombay (at present Mumbai) a youth from some semi urban place approached a saint for offering himself at the service to divine. It made the saint happy. He wanted to know the exact reason behind his stand of doing so. Saint also enquired about his capabilities and considered his offering a wise one. Actually the fellow was searching jobs in the city. He was also a normal Graduate from any sub –urban area and his financial situation was also not so good. Perhaps the sacrifice might make him temporarily happy and contented, but will become a burden in due course of time. With happiness saint suggested him for searching out a suitable job and helping the parents and inmates of the family financially. Only After gaining some wealth and knowledge the person can really enjoy the glory of sacrifice. Right now the person has nothing special to sacrifice. Such sacrifice inflicted with sorrow and agony may put both the master and the disciple in trouble.

Even divine cannot allow any individual to put oneself and families in trouble and agony. It is the only state of contentment that helps a person during movement from the physical world to the spiritual world. Offerings of any kind and in any particular form will bring happiness.

Once upon a time, a shopkeeper had a beautiful dream. The dream was so beautiful and so perfectly understandable that he feared of sharing it with others. According to his dream the God himself wanted to visit his shop. It was winter season and more special about the time that, it was raining outside. Amidst such patchy rains he preferred opening the shop. Inmates knew it better about his firmness upon any decision. He prepared some sweet dishes, some snacks and few cakes for the strange visitor of the day. Face of God was appeared in dream and was not recognisable with any clear identification marks. "The Master must introduce himself, or may give some signal so that his poor fellow can recognise", his happiness went on increasing bit by bit.

"Can I have some snacks and a cake?" An old lady was approaching the shop with a can on her hand.

"Today, actually I've not opened the shop! If you came then please, have it."

"Guest! Some special or any usual one!" Curiosity of the old lady alarmed the shopkeeper for keeping the matter a secret one.

A cowboy was approaching holding a fruit in his right hand. "That guard is chasing me. Let me come in, please."

"But, you are already inside my shop! Anyway let me see the fellow.."

Cowboy narrated the entire incident behind the reason of his hunger. That fruit was kept aside and the shopkeeper offered him a dish full of sweets, snacks and cakes.

"Don't worry my child, I'm here with you."

The matter settled in an hour. Striking of the noon time bell of the cathedral instructed the shopkeeper to finish his meal. But, what about that strange visitor! There were no traces of such visit amidst the sprinkling of droplets in the courtyard and a shower on the roads.

Evening time visitors were a cobbler, a mason, a hawker and a vagabond. Earning was not the matter of the day that is why he offered food to all the visitors with respect. It became possible because of his happiness. At last the mind refused to support him properly. Entire day and half of the night went on waiting for the master. Ultimately the time came to stop waiting for the strange visitor. His mind was still in a motive of receiving the visitor. May be the master is trying to meet him when calmness mounts the surrounding. With such anticipation he preferred keeping the door half open.

"So nice! So sweet! Really all items were tasty.." , the masterly voice brought his happiness back in dream.

"I may visit you again and again."

Morning time dream mixed up profusely with chirping of birds and silver linings of the clouds.

"God came! Who was that? May be that boy! .. " Series of anticipations and guessing went on for few moments. The entire face of the shop keeper was glistening with happiness. It was the time for feeling the presence of the Master in any nearby position. It had developed a faith in his mind, "My Master must come and visit me again."

We cannot deny the role of a school in the life of any individual. The person gains a lot during school days. S(he) can learn how to impart oneself in the society by redefining ones role in society.

It is not the only aspect of life through which any individual gets an opportunity to expose oneself to the fundamental value system prevalent in society. One's choice factor plays a definitive role in this regard.

Cultural background of an individual is greatly influenced by the immediate surroundings. Human beings, for an example of an ordinary type, are vegetarian by nature, but omnivorous by intended vigil of gaining some essential proteins from the animal sources. Development of canine indicates the biologically and naturally assigned habit to human beings. If we aspire for remaining confined within the naturally sanctioned habits of our own then the acts and conducts related to the killing of animals for the sake of gaining essentials will definitely go at its minimum.

Killing of animals for obtaining food and medicine is perpetually inflicted with acts of animism. It also signifies the place of human beings at a definite trophic level. It has also exposed our relationship with other organisms and our dependency upon the source. We rarely make ourselves capable of trpping waves directly from the sun.

It will always reach us through the involvement of producers (such as green plants). Maintaining green plants in nature and allowing them to prosper in our surrounding is, therefore, becoming a non-avoidable activity of the system in which we are confirming our presence. The referred system also limits our ascent and conducts. Within that limit of acts and conducts any human being can explore possibilities of registering the presence of oneself by performing the duties duly assigned to the individual perfectly, perpetually and vividly.

Escapism

One cannot escape from oneself without performing duties duly assigned by the system designed for ensuring interactions of different trophic levels. If we start claiming that tigers should no be allowed to kill deer, cats should not chase rats, snakes should not feed on frogs and owls should not puncture ripe fruits then our such claims will violate the laws of nature. With certain natural instincts and for maintaining a proper balance in nature organisms ensure their definite role as per the assignments. Human beings are playing a role with some sort of exceptions. One can intend to kill deer for obtaining food, one can trap fishes, kill birds, smash snakes and chase bulls for fulfilling the need of grabbing food. With a modified vigil of registering one's presence in the cycle of energy transfer one can cultivate grains, harvest fruits and maintain mulching animals for fulfilling the requirement of food. For rest of the world the role of that human will be of a protector.

With such dual principles human beings can register the presence of oneself in between the highest and middle order of the trophic level. In another aspect we people maintain our difference from others due to our ductility, capabilities to speak, performance of exhibiting our emotions and affinity of remaining linked with others. Here comes the essence of socialisation and acculturation for the same. On the basis of such involvement in the society parents cannot escape from their duties of nourishing their children, young ones cannot escape from their duties toward elders and seniors cannot escape from their affinity of helping young ones.

Escapism of any type and any degree is the affinity of human beings for which the entire community may face sufferings, loss of trust and agony. Escapism of any type can also create individual differences, depending upon which human beings often start ascertaining one's role in society.

We cannot claim that all people make them capable enough to escape from the acts of escapism and make themselves more active, more responsible, perfectly awakened and properly adjusted.

Self Esteem

Lord Krishna instructed Arjun for gaining absolute knowledge. Yoga in action cannot work alone for giving the feeling of the presence of the Divine within the self. There requires involvement of true knowledge. Knowledge alone without any action cannot bring desired result. That is why culmination of both knowledge and action is essential for feeling the presence of a supernatural creator within the self.

The state of such feeling of the culmination of knowledge and senses can make the process of renunciation of the soul possible. Aspiration of only renunciation without acquiring knowledge and without performing duty cannot work properly. It will put an individual in a state of utter confusion. The state of Self Esteem signifies the appropriate and timely correlations in between time, effort, knowledge and skills for making the role of an individual a meaningful one in the immediate surroundings.

[1]. A Trophic livel signifies the food habit of organisms during their representation as they exhibit in a food chain. Green Plants, for example prepares their own food with the help of sunlight and secures the first position in a food chain and basic position in the food pyramid. Second trophic level is occupied by herbivores, followed by carnivores at the third.

State of Mind

Human beings have a great advantage in the form of a powerful mind. It is the guiding force depending upon which they make themselves fit for different types of performances in society. They also correlate different events taking place in the nature on the basis of their state of mind and types of knowledge duly acquired by the master of senses. Regulators of all the senses depend entirely on mind for each and every effort. It also correlates the senses and memory to redefine any strategic action in relation of situation and timely need.

Say , for an instance, we cannot sit idle simply by seeing fire in our neighbor's house, because it may invade our houses too. Similarly we cannot say no to any relief and rescue operation during any natural disaster. It may put us in trouble if we remain idle during the moments of emergency. Here lies the exactness of our mind with which it works to correlate situation, timely need and knowledge to cultivate a proper strategy.

Mind is the only place where ideals and ideals generate. Generation of such ideas and ideals directly or indirectly depend upon the knowledge base of a person. Such knowledge base again resides on the segment of skills and competences that a person duly acquired while remaining active during the period of guided learning. The kind of guided learning again depends upon the combination of masterly guides and their adherence towards any culture and tradition. The ultimate root of such culture and tradition in India is the scriptures, Vedas, Upanishads and Brahmans. Some such scriptures and epics are missing due to different reasons. Some other scriptures interpreted differently by different thinkers and in gradual succession people lost their faith on the relevance of such scriptures in modern society. Here lies a mindset with which people work to make things normal and result oriented. We all rely upon our masterly guide with an apprehension of making our presence in the society by remaining active by mind and intellect. The ultimate fate of the learning of such type inflicted with adequate scope of participation helps a learner considerably in establishing a proper balance between the knowledge and intellect.

Gita also helps an individual to understand the exact culmination of the knowledge, senses, skills and intellects with an objective of making the fellow aspirant a vibrant being inflicted perfectly with a sense of performer. Such person cannot escape from the duties, as Arjun was doing; cannot negotiate with sinners; cannot put off weapons amidst a battle field and cannot indulge in conflicts without understanding consequences.

Here one can correlate the state of mind of a doer and the kind of firmness to the duty by considering an incident which took place in a village near Tatanagar (Presently in Jharkhand, India)

Any argument related to existence or non-existence of any supreme power can be addressed suitably through absolute knowledge that we gain in our phases of learning. We have incorporated various aspects related to yoga based life for addressing major aspects of various patterns of manifestations. We also move through limits of our senses for not having capabilities of exploring things beyond the scope of our senses. Simply because of our in-capabilities, for an example, we cannot claim the non-existence of bands of energies like infrared radiation, ultraviolet radiation, magnetic forces, infrasonic and ultrasonic.

A Special Moment

Third chapter